Daily Emspirations

The Universe's Mechanics Demystified

Jay Rubin

Written by
Jay Rubin

Copyright © 2022 Jay Rubin
All Rights reserved.

Jay Rubin
Malibu, CA
jayhowardrubin@gmail.com

No part or parts of this publication may be reproduced, distributed, or transmitted in any shape or form without the prior written permission of the publisher or their designated agents.

For permission requests, sales to U.S. and international bookstores and wholesalers, please contact Jay Rubin at the above email address.

Library of Congress Control Number: 2022922161
ISBN 979-8-9871813-0-0

First Edition
10 9 8 7 6 5 4 3 2 1

Printed in the United States of America

This book is dedicated to my loving and supportive family, both biologically and the dear travelers I continue to meet along the way, who have brought me joy, knowledge, comfort and stability. Their collective energy is the inspiration and empowerment that raises my vibration and feeds my soul...

Daily Emspirations

The Universe's Mechanics Demystified

Foreword

By Ari Jacobs
Secondary Educator, Malibu High School

Day-to-day living in the modern world can be a roller coaster of a ride, to say the least. The responses that we have to our daily interactions can fluctuate from moment-to-moment, and the physical and emotional states that we are in can have a large influence on our interactions with our various environments. It is easy to get lost in this modern world unless there are teachers who channel their mastery to help guide us on our journeys. Jay Rubin is one of those teachers whose experiences have led him to share what he refers to as "Universal Mechanics."

The lessons from Spirit flow through him as he helps you see that the problems of the modern world are nothing more than issues and environments constructed, in fact, by humans. Jay's channeled writings help provide the clarity that overcomes the darkness of today by allowing us to see that the true universal nature of things flows through the planet and our minds and bodies as well. The cosmic energies, connections, vibrations and light of all things flows through us all and the mechanics Jay shares are able to help transfer this comforting knowledge to all open to receive.

There is an artificial lens that can cloud reality, and until it is removed, there can be great difficulty in seeing things clearly and using our energies correctly. This is where people and souls like Jay Rubin come in to remind us of what we already know. His insight, warmth, kindness and wisdom are to be treasured. The universe works in ways that many of us cannot envision because of so many different barriers that humanity constructs, including but not limited to our need to take care of ourselves and family, materialism, consumerism, personal success and individualism. The universal realities of the powers of connection, love, balance and our everlasting vibrations together will always be what truly guides us. If we get lost and feel it is the drive for the next Rolex or personal riches that guides our actions, the mechanics Jay shares keeps us on the path that there is a benevolence to the universe with many lessons to be learned. With this guidance, we can see that we are not merely a bulb that will someday fade, but rather we are the eternal energy in that bulb which is deeply connected to all things.

What Jay's compilation of Daily Emspirations is able to articulate is that the universe, our bodies and minds, and these realities will not only guide our own personal growth, strength, resilience and health, but it is the manifestation of these realities that will be nothing short of what saves the planet and humanity for infinite generations. Our minds, bodies, Earth and the universe are all connected treasures. Sometimes we need a tune-up to get things back to balance and in line. Look no further than the pages ahead for those physical, spiritual and vibrational realignments.

From my heart to yours with all kindness, gratitude and connection... Ari

Acknowledgments

To those who have made this accomplishment possible:

My Mom – for originally opening my eyes

My Dad – for showing the difference between the light and the dark

My Loving and Nurturing Wife Dana – for being the balancing force in my life that makes it all a joy

My Compassionate Son Tanner – for giving my life higher purpose

My Brother Randy and Sister Sophie – for being the first to teach me there was more to life than the self

My Step-Mom Sandy and God Parents Joan and Austin – for showing me that family is much deeper than a blood line

My Dearest Friends Larry and Jeremy – for teaching me faith from a young age

My Fraternity Brother Gary – for always bringing the best out of me

My Emspiring Business Partner Neil – for being a driving force for good in the world

My Ever-Present Spiritual Encourager Kevin (Wait, check that, I mean Hugh) – for always nurturing my continued spiritual growth with your own thirst for knowledge

Oscar, a Kindred Spirit and Kind Soul – For transcending barriers to teach me that while all people are created as equals, the world does not always realize this truth

Darlene, Charlene and Amanda – for sharing their true selves and gifting me the opportunity to fulfill my life's true calling

My Fellow Educator and Comrade in Arms Ari – for our shared vision for a better world and your eternal love and support

Michelle & Bobby, The Masters I Am Honored to Study With – for imparting cherished wisdom and guidance

My Soul Groups, Spirits and Guides – for always having my back and empowering my divine purpose

Preface

Daily Emspirations is an anthology of channeled writings that was inspired originally by a need to uplift a friend during a troubled time in her life. These daily texts of uplifting words from me to her lead to the compilation of a "mailing list" of other kindred spirits that I felt a calling to touch with a kind gesture and a dose of positive energy to kick off their days.

As this routine became a staple in my life and that of my circle, the suggestion was made to me that it would be beneficial for me to share what I gleaned from my Reiki-infused writing sessions with a broader audience on social media. Initially, I was resistant, as I was concerned about attuning the message's vibration to a general frequency for mass consumption. The deeper I pondered the opportunity to make a real difference by paying forward the gifts bestowed upon me with all those who are open to receive, I was able to transcend my concern and post freely, thereby aligning my actions with my intent and desired results.

Over a year of daily posts lead me to realize that I would be remiss if I were not to compile the body of the writings in the form of a book to share through other avenues. My primary desire has always been to impart what has been taught to me with not just my immediate cohort, but to create a pathway to help bring an understanding of universal mechanics to a larger audience to help lighten their earthly load and raise the collective vibration for us all.

It has been my dream from a young age to make a lasting difference in the world. I know in my heart that these messages I have been asked to carry forward are part of my journey, and I am eternally grateful for the loving support that I received along the way that made it all possible.

Relax, enjoy, and absorb the pages ahead my dear friends... Be well, Jay

Life's Earthly Endowment

The perceptions we create in our lives are an amalgamation of values we have assigned to the environment in which we reside. These insights are bestowed upon us as the guidelines for our journey and formulate our basis for interactive thought and action.

As we travel our path, we covet what we feel necessary for our success, and this perspective is aligned with the view in our mind's eye. These guiding principles are esoteric in nature and attune us to the frequency of our choosing.

Please know well that all that shimmers may or may not be gold, and we have been gifted this earthly endowment to decide life's variables on a personal level. Great joy can be found in the simplest of occasions when we are open to the intentions of their creators.

Be humble in your life's purpose, be the proof that goodness prevails above all else, and be well!

Listen With Your Soul

Deep within us resides an omnipresent knowing. This knowledge is one that allows us to always be able to trace our path back to the source of all things.

The journey we are on is one that is based on the innate master plan we have hardwired within us to guide our development on this great expedition. There will be milestones along the way to mark our progress and mentors sent to impart wisdom for our benefit.

We must be open to what the universe has to share. The information that we require will be presented to the full scope of our senses through our innate ability to receive from the source.

The benevolent voices you hear are those of the guides assembled in your soul groups to protect and watch over you. Know well that you are in a hallowed space when the divine shares its vision with you to assist in your manifestation of abundance.

Be alert, be present, and be well!

Love in Your Day

Our lives are meant to be filled with love, laughter, joy and growth. The opportunity is always at your beck and call to draw to you the positive energy that lightens your load and empowers your soul.

The choice is always yours to attune your frequency to the highest vibration available to you. Within this space you will find solace through your connection to the universal source.

The focus you share with your fellow travelers conjoins you to your surroundings and enlightens your perspective with a deeper understanding of the greater good. The beauty that permeates your senses is the communal observation that links the like-minded and elevates consciousness.

Through our innate abilities to transcend the manifested domain we rise in awareness gaining access to the portal to the unmanifested realm. This cosmic gateway is nothing more than a cessation of thought and presence of focus.

Be here and Now, be aligned with the goodness in your connected self, and be well!

Maintaining Your Elevated Vantage Point

We are here to learn, experience and grow throughout the process. The joy we are all in search of comes to us as we allow its presence to permeate our perception.

The knowledge that we are the directors of the flow of positive influences in our lives is the key to mastery. Every interaction creates a possibility of infinite reactions, and these are all within our control.

From the time we awake in the morning to the moment we drift back to a heavenly dream state, we are the masters of our earthly condition. Maintain your elevated vantage point from the penthouse view you have created for yourself.

Know well that it's all an illusion that we play out based on our perceptions. Our lives are an anthology of stories we author.

Be the writer, director and producer of your masterpiece, be the bedrock of your foundation, and be well!

The Connective Tissue of the Universe

Every step you have taken in your life has led you to this exact moment in time and space. The knowledge that your efforts have always been, and always will be a meaningful part of a master plan is the awareness of the connective tissue of the universe.

When we step back from our daily routine and raise our vision to a higher perspective, we see and feel the pulse of the collective. The understanding that we are part of something much larger than ourselves is the bliss that allows for individual peace of mind and a commonality in the universal agenda.

Through the acceptance of the connected experience, we foster the synchronicity the conjoins our thoughts and their possible outcomes. Our journey is the reason for the life we have been gifted, and its path is the shared blessing.

Be the traveler with a purpose, be the one who welcomes what's in store for your soul's growth, and be well!

The Gift of Presence

When we allow ourselves the hallowed space to look deep within, we realize that the external distractions that drain us are never truly our obligation. Know well that what we actually are is the presence that manifests our personal conscious reality.

There is a connection we have to a grander source, and this pipeline is to be nurtured as it energizes us with love and kindness. The paradox to be mastered is where our individual responsibilities end and the handoff to the collective occurs.

A focus on the Now strengthens our conduit to the zero-point energy field and thereby heightens awareness and the ability to raise our individual vibration. The frequency that is reached through this practice is the attunement to life as we create it.

Be the champion of your earthly experience, be a master of the universal process, and be well!

The Individual and the Universal

As we develop our sense of self, we bridge the gap between the individual and the universal. The foundation on which we construct our essence is one that takes its shape from our distinctive life plan conjoined with the mastery of the universe.

The fundamentals we work to understand are intended to be the core curriculum of human nature. These essential lessons are presented to us through family, friends and mentors.

Know well that the connection you feel to a sense of right and wrong is your moral barometer. The instrument was installed to aid you in navigating the intended confusion that is our earthly experience.

The school of life is a customized program to meet your every need. The acceptance that the path will not always be easy is the only way to succeed without undue pain and suffering.

Allow yourself to rise above what may appear to be senseless. It has guaranteed meaning and purpose for your growth and eventual happiness.

Be in tune with your feelings and aspirations, be aligned with the bigger picture, and be well!

The Knowledge We Seek and the Company We Keep

Who we are as travelers in the vastness of the universe is the question we are all faced with in our moment-to-moment experience. The knowledge we seek and the company we keep are the building blocks of our perception.

The formulation, understanding and acceptance of our core values constructs the anchor points on which we can rely as our true self. This founding in a personal perspective becomes our sought-after paradise.

The oasis we yearn for is no farther than in our mind's eye. We all have the power within us to build what we require to be happy and healthy.

Know well that your soul will find its way to its sacred space and surround itself with kindred spirits. The elevation of your essence to the frequency of your choosing is your gift to yourself and the others to which you align your energies on Earth and beyond.

Be content in your very being, be at peace with the path you walk, and be well!

The Magic in Front of Us

As we move through our days in what appears to be an orderly and earthly cadence, we have the opportunity to notice the extraordinary. When we allow ourselves the space we require to step back from the mundane, we are granted the vision to raise our vibration.

This heightened sense of awareness ushers in the understanding that the ability to adjust our frequency is ours to manifest. The choice to attune to the higher realm opens the portal to the perpetual universal offering of advanced insight.

When our senses become aligned to the magic in front of us, our perception of the world morphs into a waking dream-state. As we open our minds to the possibilities that abound, sights, sounds and smells become vivid and fulfill an innate need we have to connect to our environment.

As the connection deepens, a trance like state envelops our being and a true meditative state is achieved. In this space, there is no fear, anxiety or concern.

Know well that when we truly listen, we hear, and when we hear, we feel. The feelings that are brought to the forefront of our experience are the union with the source energy of the collective.

Be active in your search for the signs, be aware of the gateways that exist, and be well!

Understanding Through Love

Our lives are a great adventure, with its excitement coming from a balance of traditional school-based learning and hands on experience. As we open our minds to the interactions we manifest along the way, our tool chest fills with the instruments needed to get the job done.

The challenges we all face are knowing when to reach for the required implements and how to put them to good use. We learn the how in classrooms and from the assigned reading, but there is more that only comes to us through the interaction with our fellows.

As we allow our paths to cross with the mentors that are sent to aid us on our journey, we raise our vibration to conjoin with others on that frequency. The energy we create in this space spawns a bonding and this adherence to the energetic flow leads to a loving and caring environment.

Within the safe confines of these relationships understanding is born through the symbiosis of love. This sanctified exchange beckons in the mastery of the universe to nurture and protect the highest echelon of belief systems and individual perspective.

Know well that what you glean is yours to cherish and what you treasure is yours to share. This education is a magnificent gift that is available to all through mindfulness and compassion.

Be a motivated student to life's lessons, be the benefactor to those who welcome your kindness, and be well!

Giving of Ourselves Freely

We are all part of a societal collective, and this experience is one of a physical and energetic collaboration. The stewardship we are entrusted with is a personal endeavor to open our mind and spirit to what is laid before us.

The ability to share kind words and deeds is the connection we create with our fellows. The unsolicited gesture we extend with our actions is one that emanates from our soul.

When we rise above the need to understand the outcome of a situation, we truly give of ourselves freely. Our feelings become uninhibited leading our way through acts of kindness heightening awareness and stimulating universal well-being.

Be open to where your path leads, be the manifestation of compassion, and be well!

Every Moment is an Opportunity to Connect

Our life is intended to be a mysterious chain of events that piques our wildest interest and fulfills our soul's callings. The fact that every moment is an opportunity to connect with the unknown is a portal to universal transcendence.

We are gifted the ability to utilize the insights we glean along the way to build a network of like-minded travelers to support us on our journey. The symbiotic adventures we create are the manifestations of our master plan, as we draw from the energetic source in alignment with the blessings of other kindred spirits' life force.

Know well that your moment-to-moment choices are the platform from which you interact with the cosmos. The fulfillment of our personal agendas is a moving target that we create based on the ever-changing landscape as we perceive it.

We are truly the center of our own perceptions, while simultaneously being bound to the collective through the vast neurological network of time and space. This dichotomy of mortal versus ethereal is the nexus of Heaven and Earth.

Be the grounded inhabitant of your own karmic masterpiece, be open to the experience as it presents itself to you in all its glory, and be well!

The Greatest Gift

The greatest gift we can share with others is that of our love and compassion. This virtue comes from our heart with a pureness of intent and the blessing of our soul.

The wisdom we seek is embedded within the actions we manifest. When our purpose is clear, the path we walk leads to the destinations we envision.

The goodness in our being is a shared commodity that emanates from the source. Knowing who you are grounds and protects you and those you have the honor to call friends and family.

The elevated vibration you create attunes your essence with a frequency aligned to happiness. This deep connection to the higher realm protects and guides you as your journey evades the perspective of strife and chaos below.

Be sensible in your approach, be humble and constantly kind, and be well!

The Well From Which We Drink

The highest frequency to which we can attune our vibration is that of love. The resonance that emanates in this space transcends all others.

When we align our being with the higher realm of existence, we draw directly from the source of creation. The well from which we drink feeds our soul and connects us with our fellows.

The connection we create with those in a similar space opens the doors to the life we chose for ourselves. This acceptance of what is pure and kind is the energetic foundation for being in a state of awareness.

When mindfulness is achieved, we become a beacon for the ethereal. The lighthouse effect is one that illuminates the path for others on their journey.

Knowing what you are and how you are meant to serve brings perspective and meaning to your life. Acting on this knowledge is your calling and the key to happiness.

Be in tune with your focus, be the light you see in yourself, and be well!

The Inception of Individual Awareness

Our openness to the vibrations of our soundings is the self-governance that manifests the frequency to which we attune. The acceptance that what we see is viewed through the lenses of our choosing is the inception of individual awareness.

Through the looking glass, we are able to observe life as we wish to perceive. The baseline we have created is the modeling we use to measure what we refer to as truth.

The paradigms we construct build the foundation we adhere to as the reality known as self. This earthly anchor point is cherished as stabilizing and the known commodity we share as our epitaph.

As we elevate in our energetic experience, we rise above the firewall that buffers the manifested world we know from the unmanifested universe that supports all life as we understand it. The advancement of consciousness ushers in the mindfulness that connects our visualizations with the source.

Be aligned with your knowing, be open to what is bigger than yourself, and be well!

The Omnipresence of Loving Kindness

The energy we draw from to power our souls is manifested based on the perceptions we have and the alignment we feel with the universal source. As we open our hearts to the omnipresence of loving kindness, we rise to the pinnacle of our existence.

The knowledge that we have complete control of how we present ourselves to the world is the grounding that shifts all paradigms. This knowing affords us peace of mind and an ability to quell fear and anxiety.

Look inward to your own heart center to find connection. The tools are within you to draw the nurturing you require for health and happiness.

Every day presents its challenges with its intent on your growth. Welcome the opportunities wholeheartedly and embrace the outcomes.

Be fluid in your outlook on life, be an ambassador of kindness and peace, and be well!

A Grand Purpose

We all have a grand purpose, and that deeper meaning is determined by the path we choose. The opportunity is ours on a minute-by-minute basis to update our master plan as we see fit.

The goals we strive to achieve are as simple or as complex as we desire. The tasks that lay before us are the lessons we have in store for our experiences yet to be manifested.

The understanding that knowledge is a shared universal commodity is one that will serve you well. The concept that what you need is there for the asking is truly the only lesson you need to memorize.

As we sit in our own counsel, we nurture our innate ability to tap into the source of all things. The data of the ages resides in commonality for all to call into their presence.

Some points of light are the at the first level of the communal data bank and others require more advanced authentication. When we sit in prayer and meditation, our course becomes clear.

Know well that you have all you require. Opening the doors to the answers you seek may be as simple as focusing your divine light for illumination, or others may beg the need for advanced steps to be taken.

All in all, it is all here for you once you set your sights on your desired portal of experiential belief. Faith in something much larger than any one individual, and is the stepping stone to the known and the paths beyond.

Be aware of what you know, be vigilant and accepting of what you have not learned as of yet, and be well!

Transcendent Guidance

Our connection to the mystical forces of the universe provides the transcendent guidance we require to ground and enlighten us. The highest channel of earthly opportunity resides in the emotion of gratitude.

The act of gratefulness is one that allows us to lower our heads in reverence to a source greater than ourselves. This letting go of the human ego opens the conduit to the infinite library of ageless cosmic wisdom.

As we attune to the higher frequencies, we see why we are here, who we are meant to touch, and who is destined to provide us with the support we require to accomplish the goals we set forth in this lifetime to achieve.

Look carefully at the path you walk and know it has meaning and impact. The choices you make are the legacy you leave and the strength you bequeath to others for their journey.

Be gracious in your interactions, be kind to yourself, and be well!

The Gift of Service

The life we seek here on Earth is one meant for growth through learning. The lessons we require are part of our innate master plan.

The opportunity to serve is the gift we all have the ability to share with our fellow travelers. The ways we touch others lives is our deepest connection to the universal source.

As we move throughout our days, we become a conduit for change and betterment. The knowledge that our every action has the ability to impact another's life is a positive light and cornerstone to karmic success.

Know in your heart that your path is one destined to make a difference. Keep your sights set on what is righteous and your course will impact who you are called to support.

Be open to the callings you feel, be the champion for those in your queue to assist, and be well!

Stewards of Our Own Reality

When we consciously spend the time to open our hearts, we are gifted a connection with the environment we create. Through this epiphany we are granted the knowledge we are one with our surroundings.

This elevation to oneness that we afford ourselves bestows a sense of calm in the understanding that the universe is here for the learning and growth of all who are in line with the energy as it is intended to be received. The magnitude of this power is truly unbridled and universally available.

As citizens of our own experience, we are the stewards of our own reality. The opportunity to interact with our fellows is the gift we share through acts of kindness and gratitude.

Be the driving force that unites what is good in the world, be compassionate without question, and be well!

Framework for Your Perception

As you open your eyes in the morning, you program the day that lays before you. The intentions you set are the framework for the perception that shapes your decisions and interactions.

The connection you establish with the universal source code programs your perspective and manifests your vibratory field. The choice is yours as to the vantage point you choose to view the experiences you create.

When we escalate our being to the higher realms through a conscious decision to work our programming in a positive light, we illuminate our path with a goodness that protects us from the darkness in the world. Envisioning our personal north star affixes our being to a course set for a kinder reality.

Be the initiation of who you wish to be, be the leg up others may need to ascend, and be well!

Our Mind's Eye in Aesthetic Value

Physical objects all have a unique vibration. Every animal, vegetable and mineral is attuned to a specific frequency.

Our selected channel creates the acceptable framework for the given environment. This paradigm dictates the assessment scale for up and down, right and wrong, and good and evil.

As we have all heard, beauty is in the eye of the beholder, and every beholder is subject to their personal set of house rules. The schema that is created is one that aligns one's learned opinions to the available bandwidth of cognitive perception.

The knowing that occurs is in direct correlation to our baseline of understanding. Here is where commonality and variance dovetail to prove that we all see what we see and it all imprints differently in our mind's eye in aesthetic value.

Be mindful of distinction, be aware of its connection, and be well!

The Time is Now to Spread Goodwill and Joy

The most powerful gift you can give yourself and others is that of kindness. When you approach any situation with a smile on your face, the world knows that you are open for business to receive positive vibrations.

Making the conscious effort to see the good in your fellows attunes your frequency to a higher messaging vantage point. As you elevate your being to the upper bands of conscious reality, there is an illumination that shines through your soul for all to see.

The energy you emanate becomes a magnet for others in a similar space and is amplified through your interactions. The knowledge that your relationships are the connection by which your light is expressed is a catalyst for universal benefit.

The time is Now to spread goodwill and joy. You have the tools, the time and the talent.

Be an enthusiastic agent of exhilaration, be the light that people turn to for happiness, and be well!

Letting Go of Quantitative Thinking

The sun comes up and the sun goes down and what happens in between is gravy! Western philosophic thought puts a heavy premium on the value of time as we perceive it in the manifested space.

The watches we strap to our arms become not just a time-telling device, but a tether to the earthly realm. We know in our hearts that we are not beholden to anything but our own ability to connect with our environment on the frequency of our choosing.

When we rise above the confusion that permeates our world, we are able to feel the vibration of the universe that allows for all the goodness we are here to receive. There is no true evaluation you can place on the moments of your life.

The ability to be in the present is a priceless gift to be cherished. Letting go of quantitative thinking is the key to creating a qualitative energetic flow. This grounding creates a peace of mind that transcends time and space.

Be attuned to the cosmic clock, be aloof to a constraining construct, and be well!

Time Spent in the Light

There are many of us who grow up with a deep understanding of our life's purpose and others who may spend their lives searching. There is little difference energetically betwixt the two as long as your time is spent in the light with positive intentions guiding your path.

For those on the active journey to open themselves to enlightenment, the road is one that beckons the lessons required to shape perspective and raise vibration. The truth we seek is a personal one, requiring a general acceptance of self-worth and faith in the greater good.

The moment your dendrites connect and your synapses fire in such a way that the gift of a deeper knowing becomes evident to you, a smile will come to your face, immediately followed by a calm in your heart. This captivating connection will become your homeostasis forevermore.

Know well that the experience that is your life is unfolding according to plan. You have always known what you know and when you are truly ready you will be prepared to know it all.

Be calm in your growth, be the expanse that bridges the gap, and be well!

The Magic of Connection

There are days where we feel we are in the groove, like nothing can stop us from accomplishing anything and everything, and there are some days where we aren't quite as in sync as we would like to be. This alignment we strive for is the magic of connection.

When we recognize and acknowledge the mystical force within us that connects us with the source of all power and understanding, we are granted access to the infinite wisdom and drive of the universe. This gift is one that you always have the ability to grant yourself in the present moment.

The acceptance that we are all part of the same neurological network is the game-changing paradigm that awakens consciousness and ignites your drive to excel. Release your spirit from its blinders and experience life as it's intended to be.

Look carefully at what you have manifested, and know what has been created is meant to support your travels. Pay homage to who you are though your realization that the simplest things you take for granted are the magical fibers that tie you to the grander scope of reality.

Be the magician of your intentions, be in awe of what you see, feel and know in your heart, and be well!

Molding Our Inner Consciousness

Our lives are our opportunity to create the essence of being we chose to experience. The gift we grant ourselves is the understanding of how we interconnect with the grander plan.

As we shape our perceptions, we build the connections that energize our reality. The outward emanation of our vibration molds our inner consciousness and attunes to the perceived frequency of our life's purpose.

Our very presence becomes a beacon for the standards we uphold. The banner we fly beckons others of the same ilk.

The nexus of camaraderie we create with like-minded souls constructs the foundation of our design. These building blocks are the structural DNA that binds our karmic purpose with our earthly construct.

Know well that you are the masterful project of your own architecture. Enjoy the artistic license you have been granted, as the possibilities are infinite.

Be the blank canvas you were intended to be, be the artwork you see in your mind's eye, and be well!

The Tribe We Assemble

The goals we seek are illuminated by the brilliance of the trajectory in our mind's eye. As we expeditiously set our sights on the dreams to be manifested through active and deeper connection, our life purpose takes its course.

The tribe we assemble brings with it stability and comfort. This opportunity to share time and space with kindred souls opens our thought processes to the vast possibilities that are our world.

The joy that comes from intellectual advancement is supported by circumstance and societal growth. When we learn, we flourish, and as we expand our being, we continue to attract others in like vibration.

The frequency we attune to beckons to us those we love. The blessing we are gifted with is the creation of an extended family to be cherished.

As we survey in retrospect the great endowment our life has afforded us, we come to realize that our truest pleasures have come from what we have experienced and who we were able to share it with as our days passed. Happiness was, is and will always be there for our enjoyment as we remain open to the newness all around us.

Be grateful to be enrolled in the school of life, be the student of your design, and be well!

Transcendence Through Daily Routines

The essence of our being is deeply rooted in our connection to the universal source. The knowledge that we are all part of an eternal oneness is the connective tissue that links our collective body and spirit.

As we continue on our path of transcendence through our daily routines, we manifest the lessons we require to fulfill our life's goals. The experiences we are blessed with are ordained as the puzzle pieces that fit together to create our whole.

Know well that you are a work in progress, and your personal joy comes hand in hand with the acceptance of what you consent to as your truth. The meaning of your journey is as significant as you choose and your perception is the anchor of your reality.

Be honest with your intentions and actions, be consistent with your energetic allocations, and be well!

The Application of the Gems We Collect

We enter the world with a baseline understanding, and are expected to build upon that innate human wisdom. The opportunity to share in the beauty of our lives is the education we all are afforded as part of the general admission experience.

Every waking moment is a gift to be cherished and put to good use. The lessons come to us in all shapes and sizes to be stored in long term memory.

The application of the gems we collect are the tools we covet for use when called upon. The knowledge arrives not merely as just the function, but the means by which we apply its usefulness along the way.

The route we travel is designed to grow us as souls working toward a grander purpose. The goal of transcendence to a deeper understanding of a higher existence is a never-ending endeavor.

Know in your heart it all has purpose, and in retrospect this will become apparent. Trust in your path and your path will lead you home.

Be the student of life in all its glory, be ever coachable, and be well!

The Road to Elsewhere

So much of our lives are spent searching for who we are and where we are supposed to go. We are generally taught that the path to success is one that starts within us and leads to external gratification.

The road to elsewhere is a never-ending highway that leads to disappointment. Look no farther than your own heart center for the connection you need to fulfill your life purpose and wildest dreams.

The knowing that your positive relationship to the source is all that you require to fill your soul and empower your life is the catalyst for enlightenment. Through this mindfulness, we allow our vibration to attune to the highest frequency available to us.

Be centered and connected in your power, be aligned with the grander perspective, and be well!

Your Personified Space

The environment in which we reside is the shelter we manifest from our innermost beliefs. The energy we draw from to shape our experience is the essence of our being.

Know well that your journey is a pilgrimage for your soul's contentment. This odyssey will twist and turn, but will always lead you home.

As you create your personified space, you influence those around you with your life force's power and compassion. Your mindfulness is the determining factor as to the heights you will reach in peace of mind and consciousness.

Be the artwork in the gallery of your existence, be the light on pathway for your kindred spirits, and be well!

Allocation of Presence

The world in which we live is one that puts a high reverence on our ability to multitask to maximize our earthly countenance. The challenge we all face is having the will and the courage to focus our energy on what lays before us, allowing for an optimization of our output based on the frequency to which we attune.

The essence of our being can easily be subdivided between the objects and outcomes of our choosing. The output we generate is wholeheartedly dependent upon our allocation of presence, and its end results will be in direct correlation to complexity of the equation we manifest.

Know well that when you look deeply into someone's eyes you create a connection. This oneness aligns your auric fields with the source and brings unbridled power to your disposal.

This same connectivity awaits the individual who hones their attention on any given circumstance. There is no limit to what one can do when there is focus of mind and body on spirit.

Be 100% in your doing, be the force that moves mountains with your will, and be well!

Creating a Calm, Sustainable Existence

There is a balance that we all seek in our lives that creates a calm, sustainable existence. This work in progress is our life's mission and when we look no farther than our present moment we are able to recognize we have all we need.

Please know that what we achieve in a state of presence is connection to the deepest of understandings. The omnipotence is the realization that when we allow ourselves to simply be, the stresses of what might be fade away into the ether.

The Now holds your individual power, creativity and joy in alignment with the source. This single point in time is the portal to the vast database of universal knowledge.

Release your concerns by clearing the clutter that clogs your mind. Know in your heart that you are on the right path, and continue to follow the vision of your dreams.

Be unwavering in your pursuit of kindness and compassion, be the strength you willfully share with those in need, and be well!

The Fuel You Require to Power Your Soul is Free of Charge

There is a direct correlation between the velocity at which we live our lives and the quality of the life we live. Our mental and physical engines only get so many revolutions, and it's up to us to determine the rate at which we expend our life force.

Know well that the fuel you require to power your soul is free of charge. The only expenditure to you comes in the form of acceptance; acceptance of what is and what is meant to be, based on your life goals and the interactions with your cohort's kindred spirits.

The frequency to which you are attuned sets your observed environment to the sensory inputs aligned to the vibratory field of your manifestation. As we slow our pace, we limit the physical data points we absorb, allowing for a deeper saturation of the healing energies that surround us.

The love is literally in the air if you take the time to create a symbiosis with the universal source. This immersion is the zen we all seek and it is entered Here and Now...

Be present in your observations, be aligned with what you know, and be well!

The Goodness We Have in Our Lives

The energetic bonds we have with our family and friends nurtures and sustains us. This symbiosis is the connection we have with the universe and all the goodness we have in our lives.

This bidirectional experience is the shelter we create that protects and guides us. When we open ourselves to the kindness that the world is offering in return for our attention, the tumblers align and the doors to understanding open.

Compassion and kindness are the olive branches we are blessed to offer to our kindred spirits. These gestures of goodwill attune our vibrations with those we love and care about on our journey.

The ability to create relationships based on love and mutual respect are the cornerstones of happiness. Please know well that all we truly have is each other, and this knowledge is the most cherished of all knowing.

Be open to what feels right in your life, be the smile on your face and others, and be well!

Be Playful in All You Do

The focus we gift to our lives is the present that we share with ourselves and those lucky enough to be in the concentric bands of our energetic experience. Know well that the energy we are blessed to allot to our fellows is drawn directly from the source, and we merely act as a conduit for its transmission.

As we mature, we are taught that life becomes more serious and outcomes more astringent. This school of thought is antiquated, and no longer served the higher purpose.

The new paradigm works diligently to bring to light that our purpose is one that dovetails neatly with the same kindness and compassion we were taught as youngsters. The illumination that shines on us in our youth is not lost in adulthood or beyond.

There is always a place in our hearts for the connection to the things that bring happiness to our being. The labels we are taught limit our perception and therefore our ability to allow joy to find its way to us.

By using feelings to deepen our understanding of the grander scope, we elevate our consciousness above earthly limitations. Our activities all have purpose and these meanings all engage an opportunity for growth.

There is no reason to ever stop playing the game you live. We are here to learn, and there is no better way to enhance yourself than to brighten your path with what you love.

Be playful in all you do, be a kid at heart no matter your age, and be well!

Repel the Negative and Beckon the Positive

Our outward disposition is a choice for us to make based on our inward perception. The magnification of the frequency we select to emanate is how we present to our fellow travelers.

The knowledge that the core of our being is amplified through our presence in any situation is the portal to universal connection. The ability to determine the cohort of our choosing is truly an act of mindful energetic selection.

The physical space and persons you overtly choose to share your consciousness with are the energy repeaters of your vibration. The decision on companionship is paramount for your happiness and well-being, as we are extensions of our environment.

Take careful inventory of where to go and with whom you associate. Your auric field is boosted or depleted through interaction.

Know well joy is truly self-manifested and you have the tools to achieve this pinnacle. Trust in your instincts to repel the negative and beckon the positive.

Be a magnet for kindness, be a beacon of light, and be well!

No Two Days are the Same by Design

Our lives are a delicate balancing act of our energetic output, solely dependent on personal prioritization. The choices we make all play an integral part in the allocation of our physical bandwidth and the maintenance of our well-being.

If we look at ourselves holistically, we can envision a pie chart of our activities adding up to 100%. The life quest we are on is to manifest an alchemy that generates a homeostatic environment.

The goal is to solve the equation that weighs our requirements and desires in an equal fashion. Not all of us maintain the same quotient, as the calculations differ from soul to soul.

What remains constant in us all is the need for a buffer from the red zone where we surpass our ability to function at our peak performance. This burstable space where there is capacity to absorb the ebb and flow of life's ever-changing challenges is paramount to upholding stability and fluid functionality.

Know well that no two days are the same by design to ensure new inputs to our growth process. It is our task to stand vigilant in the protection of our own health and happiness though active participation in setting the success criteria.

Be the engineer of your own balance, be one with the variables that make you unique, and be well!

All Roads Lead Home

The deep connection we have to our core beliefs stems from our innate life plan. This curriculum we have hardwired from birth is our earthy opus in the making.

The knowledge that we have set out with a goal as our life focus is the path we have chosen to follow. There is no possible true deviation as all roads lead home.

The connection we create with our fellows is the love we have to share. As we extend our hand in kindness to help others, we nourish our soul in alignment with the grander scheme.

We are all works of art in progress to be cherished. The ability to delve within ourselves to expand the bandwidth at our disposal works on a sliding scale based on momentary necessity.

We are here to foster universal goodness, and the universe in kind supports us on our mission. The energetic transference of the circle of life is a constant for us to behold in awe, as it stimulates growth, compassion and understanding for those open to receive.

Be the active catalyst of your own transcendence, be the sponsor of karmic outreach, and be well!

Life's Syllabus

Our days are filled with moments of interaction and introspection. These opportunities are all gifted to us as the lessons we requested in our master plan.

Know well that your waking hours are yours to guide as you traverse the landscape before you. The people you meet and the places you travel to are all a part of the course work in your personal syllabus for life.

The journey we create is one we balance between the Earth and ethereal plane of existence. The days we manifest are the interactive classroom of our design, and our dream state is the cosmic review session with our soul groups and guides.

When we align our path with our goals we feel a symbiosis in purpose. The connection to our desired state of being fosters inner peace and happiness.

Be grateful for your teachers and classmates, be the student that your life intends you to be, and be well!

What More There Is

The life we set out to live is artistry in the making from the day we are born to the inevitable transcendence to the grander heavenly connection. Our experience has no manifested boundaries, no timeline, and no limitations we were not created to surpass.

As we travel the road, we build one stepping stone after another, and we come to realize that the illusory concept of time is a fleeting notion constructed to manifest a baseline for urgency. This false truth is a low-level vibrational perception that is overcome within your personal presence.

The bonds we forge with our fellow travelers are the mooring tethers we are gifted with as grounding tools for interaction. The knowledge that we are not alone on Earth fosters the larger questions into what more there is and what more is expected of us.

There is an energy, a knowing we all seek that completes us. This sought-after calm is one that is inevitably found in the connected state of Love.

Be of open heart and soul, be a transcendent point of human focus, and be well!

A Successful Pilgrimage

As we travel our path, we have a cadence we set, and this rhythm is attuned to the vibrational alignment of our life purpose. This frequency is the emanation we share with our cohort and the band on which we receive.

The intentions we set for our journey are conscious in nature and are the framework for our existence. This mindful undertaking opens our soul to the lessons we seek.

Know well that all we require for a successful pilgrimage is of our own creation. This self-realization is the gateway to transcended thought and action.

Be honest, be faithful, and be well!

We All Came Here with a Purpose

We all came here with a purpose, a goal to make a difference. The change we plan on fashioning may be one of personal growth, or it may be global in magnitude.

The essence of our being is steeped in energy, and this life force is an extension of the grander scope of universal power. Know well that your personal agenda is part of the larger cosmic scope, and should always be looked at with such reverence.

Look no farther than your own hopes and dreams to find your deeper meaning and the ability to make a mark on ledger of life's accomplishments. This hallowed space you call your life has profound depth and a grand role in the path that unfolds before us all.

Know well that the space you hold is as clear as you make it and that your effect will be felt by all you touch. The role you play is one to be cherished, as it's yours to nurture and bring to life's stage.

Be the person you have always known you are, be the headliner in your experience, and be well!

Our Innermost Feelings

Our innermost feelings are the manifestations of our soul plans aligning with the earthly circumstances we encounter. These emotions are the conduit by which we bring our energetic experience to life.

As we use our senses to input the data we receive, we realize that there is more than we can tangibly perceive. This knowing deepens our perspective and opens our heart to the vast expanses of universal wealth.

The sounds of birds in the trees by a running creek, the smell of the dew on the morning grass and the smile on a child's face are all signs that there is something that conjoins us all. This deeper understanding is the gateway to the connectivity that empowers our being.

Know well that your essence is grander than what lays before you. The connection you have with your environment is one that connects you to the frequency of Love.

This channel of attunement will heighten your senses, expand your scope of manifested understanding and enlighten your very presence to the unmanifested spirit.

Be what you feel, be the light in your world, and be well!

The Reality We Bring to Our View

The perspective we all have on life is the reality we bring to our view. This manifestation is of our choosing, and its scope is the breadth of our possible interaction.

This frequency to which we attune is the band of our life force's possible resonation. This realm of creation is as pliable as we choose it to be.

There is no set vibration for our life's path. The travels we choose are the stories we will have to share.

As we journey, we select the halls of our experience. The hallowed exchanges we have the honor to learn from along the way ebb and flow with our needs in accordance with our master plan.

When you reach a fork in the road, you have choices gifted to your mind's eye. These opportunities are the chapters of your visions to behold.

Know well that your tales are yours to bring to life and your dreams are the source. The power of the universe is at your disposal with kindness, compassion and gratitude as your guide.

Be above the fray, be the light others look to lead the way, and be well!

The Signpost of Compassion

Every day is a new opportunity to work toward the goals that we have charted as a roadmap for earthly success. There are some that see more traction than others, but it's always our attitude that determines our true progress.

The knowledge that the milestones are within reach is the wind in our sails. The acceptance of the space we are currently in is what allows us to make the best of any situation by creating the positive energy that we draw from to motivate our family and friends.

Our goals are the ever-present destinations we have plotted on the map. Please know life has an interesting way of making the detours that take us where we truly need to be.

Make the best of what is handed to you and you will always be at the exact right mile marker. Please never lose sight of the fact that the joy comes in helping others along the road.

Be the signpost of compassion others seek on their travels, be the smile that warms hearts and lightens loads, and be well!

The Soundtrack of Our Design

Our lives are a work of art that we create through our intentions and interactions. This masterpiece is the feature film that we have the honor of playing the lead role in as well as serving as the executive producer.

The script is one that we bring to life based on our grander plan and the relationships we draw into our auric field. The beauty of the experience is amplified by our perception of the outcomes of our daily existence.

We have the opportunity to set the tempo of our very being to the soundtrack of our design. The music is all around us in the forms of laughter, birds singing and loved one's voices.

Look no farther than the stage you have created for your happiness. The music of our own pageantry is the manifestation of our core essence and its inner magical connection with the universe.

Be listening to all you hear, be the concerto of your own consciousness, and be well!

Embrace the Practice

Our lives are filled with tasks to accomplish and joys to be remembered. No matter the order of the experiences, we can rest assured that one day after the next will be occupied with items, issues and inquiries requiring our attention.

Embrace the practice with an eagerness to accomplish what is laid before you. Know well that the lessons learned are the fruit of your tree of life, and they are to be savored in all of their sweetness and sometimes sorrow.

Grant yourself the strength to meet each day with the energy and desire to be in the thick of it all, never putting off what can be accomplished today because tomorrow's dance card looks open. Draw your power from today's path and the light it shines!

Be the embrace that sees today as a gift, be the joy in your loved one's lives, and be well!

Our Highest and Best Purpose

The path we walk is one that guides our life journey as we travel toward our highest and best purpose. This expedition is one we set out to accomplish from birth with the guidance of our family, friends and soul groups.

The knowledge that there is a greater good that envelops us all is the protection we all rely on as the true north that illuminates the way. Our travels are never without opportunity to shed light on the unknown and to bring a new and enlightening perspective to our being.

The teachers we are blessed with on our journey are the beacons sent to us to raise our consciousness, create mindfulness and fill our souls with love and light. These outstretched hands of kindness remind us we are not alone and that our goals are never too lofty to be brought to fruition.

Every interaction is a blessed event in the making. Every traveler we encounter along the way is a mirror of our own perception, sent to grant introspection on the depth of our well-being.

Know well you are never alone on your quest. The powers of the universe are forever at your side.

Be conscious of your kindness, be the manifestation of good will, and be well!

Our Power and Knowledge

Our power and knowledge are drawn from the ability to stay above the fear and unrest that life's lessons have a way of manifesting for our own growth and transcendence. The circumstances that come across our paths are not always of our creation, nevertheless we always have control of our reactions.

When we practice staying centered we realize that what is needed to succeed is not within the drama du jour, it is in the deeper understanding of the bigger connected picture. Look within to find your strength and connectivity to the universal source to rise above the face value of the Earth-bound learning experience.

When a challenge arises, this is an opportunity to utilize your introspective skill sets to determine what your true relationship is with the situation at hand. The data you glean from this profound understanding will open your mind as well as show you the path to share with those you love.

Be brave, be always mindful, and be well!

Life is a Rhythmic Flow

Life is a rhythmic flow of energy that powers our spirits and connects us with the lessons we require to grow and flourish. These opportunities come to us in the form of experiences and the teachers we manifest into our presence.

Our days resemble a rushing river with all of its perceptual beauty and peril. The act of casting off the mooring line and allowing your vessel to traverse the unforeseen waters is the acceptance that fosters your ability to mature into the person you choose to be.

We have choices; we always have choices. These options are the baseline decisions we make to attune our vibrations to the frequency that we require to become our best selves.

The knowledge that acceptance of what life has in store for us is the key to opening our very being to the resources we desire for a tranquil existence on a path to transcendence. This knowing mitigates fear and elevates our essence to a higher vantage point where what we seek becomes clear and readily attainable.

Be courageous in your pursuits, be wise in your interpretations, and be well!

Free Yourself

The situations of our lives are not black and white, as there are always multiple lenses to view every state of affairs. Stepping back and taking an objective perspective frees us from the canned responses and knee-jerk reactions we use as defense mechanisms to protect ourselves from pain.

Elevating your view will allow for new tools to be built and paradigms to be put into play. Trust that your tool box has all of the necessary equipment required to build the infrastructure needed for a successful journey.

You have all you need at your disposal to not just do the job at hand, but to be truly successful at it. Trust in your ability and the kindness of your cohort to support your endeavors and dreams.

Be awakened in your perspective, be open to what comes, and be well!

The Looking Glass We Cherish

The perception that is our life is the amalgamation of our life's experiences and the theme of our soulful master plan. The viewfinder of our mind's eye is the looking glass that we cherish as we create the visions of our reality.

What lays before us is an illusion of our creation steeped in the consciousness we manifest. This understanding holds a powerful outcome for all who venture to let go of what tethers them to what they think they know, and opens their thoughts to the vastness of their dreams.

Know well that your world is of your expression, and that your story unfolds as you so choose. The magnificence that you hold in your heart is the canvas for your artistry, and your will to live the brushes, paints and loving light that bring it all to fruition.

Be your wildest dreams come true, be true to your knowing, and be well!

Having a Purpose

Having a purpose gives us perspective for the allocation of our personal energies. The desire to make a difference in someone's life is an endeavor that can easily start with a kind thought.

Our positive intent is the springboard that ignites the engines of kindness and change. Starting small is the first step in building toward any bigger dream you have in your mind's eye.

Simply lending a hand to someone in need, or an ear as a sounding board can be the origination point of a process that could alter the course of history. You never know what grand outcome will be reached by the simplest of gestures, a kind word or even a caring smile.

Do your part knowing well that the scope of your immediate contribution is never too small to make a difference. It's all part of the bigger picture to help one another achieve our life plans.

Be the one who others can count on for compassion, be the joy we all need, and be well!

Listen to What You See

Acceptance is the key. It truly is as simple as that!

When we allow ourselves the latitude to ebb and flow with the circumstances we are presented with, we find a rhythm, and this cadence creates a symbiosis with our environment that manifests peace of mind. This state of understanding of what is becomes the grease on the tracks that simplifies our existence as we live without undue friction and stress.

Within this state of being resides a deeper tranquility that aligns with our life plan and ushers in the experiences that are best suited for our growth and transcendence. The lessons we require are presented as the gifts they are intended and their teachings absorbed without delay.

Our path is our journey and we choose its twists and turns. The greater our ability to let go, the straighter the road traveled.

Listen to what you see, and see what you hear. Know well it all has purpose and your best interest at heart.

Be the magnification of your spirit's purpose on Earth, be a positive influence on others in your world, and be well!

Creative Being

We are all creative beings by nature with our own personal processes to bring our ideas to fruition. Some of us need silence to foster inspiration, while others need all of their dendrites and synapses firing with external stimulation like loud music or white noise.

The goal is simple, allow yourself the kind of space you require to connect with the creativity within where you draw your emspiration! Have faith in your method; that's what makes artistry come to life.

Know well that you are the master of your experience, and your connection to the grander source will allow you to manifest your dreams into reality. The kindness in your heart is intended to soothe your soul so you can amplify your essence to the world in which you reside.

Be the creativity you require, be the spark for others understanding, and be well!

Currency of Kindness

As we journey through our lives, we are blessed with the opportunity to interact with people from all walks of life while sharing time and space. The investments we make in these relationships becomes the currency of kindness that lights our way.

Some of the connections we make last a lifetime, and others are short term experiences. No matter the duration of the energy exchanged, it is always intended for the betterment of us all.

The goodwill that we all share has a cumulative effect that builds in the reservoirs of the energetic fields that bond us all on Earth. As this conduit fills with positive life force, we gain a sense of joy that raises spirits and lightens the collective load.

Know well that when you act in accordance with the goodness that mindfulness fosters, you do a universal service. This deeper understanding is the knowledge you disseminate to raise the ocean for the grander benefit.

Be aligned with your essence, be conscious of your connection, and be well!

Putting Yourself First

There is a common misconception that putting yourself first is a selfish and narcissistic perspective on life. Please know that there is nothing farther from reality.

The ability to nurture one's self is the cornerstone of personal health and happiness. The understanding that we are the core of our being is the conduit to a grander scope of connection and enlightenment.

When we bless ourselves with our own attention to growth, love and gratitude, we become open to the fruits of the universe. The energy that bonds us emanates from our heart center, and through this portal we connect with others on a similar path.

The vibration we attune to selects the frequency we absorb. The metaphysical process is furthered by our amplification of this energetic experience as we act as an antenna connecting like-minded souls in thought, feeling and action.

Be kind to yourself, be kinfolk to your fellows, and be well!

Purposeful, Meaningful and Enjoyable

The life we live is designed to be purposeful, meaningful and enjoyable. The choice is ours to create a life paradigm that manifests happiness and growth.

The opportunity to experience the lessons we desire as part of our master plan is readily available to us, and its path is one we build as our days unfold. The interactions we draw to us are the visions we hold in our hearts, and we are the catalyst for their very being.

Know well that your power is derived from a deeper connection. This sense of bonding with the universe is the oneness that brings love and light into your essence.

Be attuned to your larger purpose, be the flow that enlightens your presence, and be well!

Energy Flows Like Water

Energy flows like water as does our lives. The power that bonds all living things works in harmony to create a universal symbiosis.

The experience we are all blessed with is one that is custom made for our growth and well-being. The knowledge that we are exactly where we are meant to be is the grounding we can rely on for stability.

The course we take and the interactions that are generated are designed to support our higher purpose. Resistance to what is creates a logarithmic friction in the time space continuum that manifests within us as pain and sorrow.

Allowing events to play out without discourse directly connects our desires with the grander scheme. When we align with the energetic position of our surroundings, we become one with the natural order and reap the highest benefits from the opportunity.

Be accepting of what is, be content with being, and be well!

Cultivation of the Divine

Our ability to connect to the source is a factory-installed birthright. The protocol to plug into the vastness of the universal network is un-password protected in the higher realm.

The knowing that connection comes from deep within us is the key to unlocking unbridled power and knowledge. Transcendence to this space comes of a still mind that is achieved during meditation and prayer.

The environment in which the collective expanse can be reached is one that must be nurtured. The cultivation of the divine is best achieved through quieting one's physical environment, thus fostering the energetic flow from the zero-point energy field.

The absence of the distraction of earthly noise focuses the process on the frequency akin to our vibration. Without the externality of other sources our ascension's mapping is completed.

The inducement of this portal opens our abilities far beyond the what we knew we could achieve in a disconnected state of being. What we gain is clarity of mind and soul.

Be at peace in your sanctified space, be one with the magnification of what the silence bestows, and be well!

Our Own Design

We are all creatures of our own design. The path we walk is one that we create based on our need to grow as we expand our consciousness.

The ability to connect with our environment is a gift to be cherished as our enlightened sense of awareness evolves. Our awakening is nurtured by the kindred spirts we welcome into our lives.

The perceptions we manifest are the interpretations that we have built in alignment with our life plan and the lessons learned in the classroom of our experiences.

Know well that what you know is what you feel, and what you feel is what you know. This balance is your gateway to self-acceptance and tranquility.

Be at peace as you search for reality, be kind to yourself on the journey, and be well!

Conscience Living and Connection

We are all the manifestation of our design. The planning we put into who we wish to be is the amalgamation of our life experiences and the vision we set out to create.

Every moment of every day is an opportunity to better our being through conscious living and connection. The journey we are on sees our path intersect with the experiences and souls we are blessed to share time and space with.

The joy is ours to derive and the lessons ours to learn. The knowing is the gift and the chance to share is the challenge.

Allow yourself to freely live your life as you see it in concordance with the reality of your choice. The harmony you will feel is the universe shining back on you that which you have granted your eternal self.

Be one with your purpose, be open to what others offer along the way, and be well!

Amplifier for Kindness

The energy we exude is the vibration to which we attune. This frequency is the alignment between our physical and conscious selves.

The radiance of our essence is the connection we have with the universe. Know well that our choices are the catalyst for all things that we beckon into our auric experience.

When we open our minds, our awareness grows into an enthusiasm for life and all it has to offer us on our journey. This mindfulness becomes a joy in the understanding of the mechanics of how the cosmos works to align all aspects of time and space.

Be an amplifier for the kindness all around you, be the positive force that others can depend on to help light their way, and be well!

Cosmic DNA

Throughout the ages, people have contemplated the answers to life's grander meaning. This quest has been the launching point for many of the great thinkers in human history.

As we have evolved as a species, we have gained complexity in our societal structure and technological ability. Through this process, we have wandered farther and farther away from what matters most: our ability to feel the connection to the life force that is all around us.

The purpose we all seek is within ourselves. No two individuals share the exact same intentional essence or plan to accomplish the goals in their minds' eye.

We all have a life plan. This inner blueprint resides in our karmic records like cosmic DNA. Please know that no action is preordained, but your higher-level agenda was something that you installed within yourself like firmware upon reentry into this incarnation.

The ability to tap into the energetic mana that surrounds us is a gift we bestow upon ourselves through mediation and prayer. Take the time to plug in through the metaphysical outlets of your choosing.

The manifested world in which we live is equipped with the equivalent of free Wi-Fi for all those with a desire to transcend. The network's password is simply the active passion in what you do and how you believe.

Be an antenna for what flows all around us, be one with your vibration, enhance the amplitude you emanate, and be well!

A Sense of Knowing

There is a sense of knowing that we all experience as we travel the path that is our life. This understanding is the deep connection we all share within our core that adjoins our life purpose with the collective universal consciousness.

The feelings we have are the manifested process that bonds the fibers of the universe and maintains the cosmic superhighway that connects us in time and space. Our thoughts lead to action, and this interaction with others creates the reactions that brings forth the metamorphosis that elevates the overarching environment.

Know well that you come well equipped with the tools and fortitude to bring your desired growth into being. Trust in your inner feelings of intention; this dedication always serves on a grander scale.

Be passionate about your creation, be compassionate to others in your space, and be well!

Above Thinking

Truth is the understanding of our perception. This reality is conceived from a deep knowledge that emanates from vibration.

The energetic experience that resonates from situational interaction sets the framework for our alignment with frequency. When we allow the attunement we achieve to become the lens of our perspective, we gain a connection to the higher realm.

The path we walk in the upper spaces grants the view that opens our minds to a collective certainty. This place of simply being at peace with all things bridges the gaps between wonder and knowing.

Reassurance comes to those who let go of their thoughts and relinquish the reigns to their intuition. The prevailing force of the universe awaits when you tie into the power that is above thinking; it resides in feeling.

Be open to your insights, be a conduit for life's energy, and be well!

You Are Never Alone

The vantage point we take in life is the platform from which we see what lays before us on our journey. This hallowed ground is deep within our soul and connects us to the goodness that is meant for us all.

As we learn and grow, we come to the realization that we are not unaccompanied on our adventure. The friends and family we have assembled are here to aid us along the way.

The acceptance that it is always a team effort lifts the veil between our experience and that of our fellow travelers. This connection magnifies the energy we wield, as we realize the power that the universe offers in alignment with our essence.

Rest well knowing that you are never alone on your travels. Our path is one that allows for many landscapes and outcomes, all with our best interest at heart.

Be the shining beacon you follow home, be the person you set out to be, and be well!

The Space is Open

The environment in which we live is seen through the lens we are attuned to perceive. This space is as open or constricted as we allow it to be based on the inherent understanding of our safety.

The ability to connect with the energy that surrounds us is a gift granted to those who have elevated their consciousness above fear and found security in their knowing. The understanding that all will be provided as needed in a mindful state is the endowment for those on a journey of transcendence.

As we climb, our eyes open and the view becomes clear. Our purpose follows closely and the deeper meaning of it all brings a smile to our souls.

The power to create is what shines through the vastness. The insights gained through this conduit are the magnification of the universal source to benefit collective goodness.

Be in alignment with what you feel, be open to bringing it to life through your kindness of action, and be well!

The Construct of Our Intentions

The energy we allocate to the needs of our environment is ever-dependent on the focus we grant to the situation at hand. The conscious awareness we bestow is the mindful attunement to the wholeness of our being.

The essence we manifest of our presence is the bandwidth we align to the representative pie chart we bring into reality. This construct of our intentions is our earthbound resonance.

Know well that your allotment of self is your gift to share with the world. This extension of your essence is in constant flux depending on your needs and desires.

Be aware of what is essential to your happiness and the requirements of those around you, be the one who gives of yourself fully without concern, and be well!

Evolution and Awakening

The essence of who we are is like a fingerprint we leave on everything we touch. The blessings that we share with the world come in the form of our actions, words and intentions.

The goals we strive toward and the achievements we accomplish all emanate from the vibration we manifest. The frequency to which we attune connects us with others on a similar path.

As like-minded mindful souls amass in thought and location, the vibration of the world is elevated. This transcendence is what some refer to as evolution and others as awakening.

The ability to allow your inner light to guide you is the freedom we all seek. This autonomy grants the true gift of awareness.

Be blessed in your being, be mindful of what you mean to the world, and be well!

The Cosmic Dance

The days we live embody the magic we create. The manifestation of our being is our consciousness coming to life before our very eyes.

The opportunity to bring forth the visions we seek is the gift we grant ourselves. The world we know is the one of our willingness to simply be who we set out to be as our essence aligns with our life's purpose in form and magnitude.

There is no act of kindness or interaction with our fellows that is too small to be recognized as a moment to be held in gratitude. The opportunity to be part of the cosmic dance we call life is the symphony that we all conduct.

This mastery is the spirit of our being as it conjoins with the paths of others. Know well it all has purpose in your grand plan, and that you are a catalyst for more than meets the eye.

Be true to where your heart leads, be open to mindfulness as your awareness grows, and be well!

Successful Completion

"There is no time like the present" is an age-old adage that resonates as a common motivational statement to combat procrastination. If you look a little deeper into its meaning you will see that not only is there no time like the present, but there is no other time but presence.

We are all on the mission du jour that we have set forth to accomplish. The focus we are able to conjure is the key to its successful completion.

The energy we allot to any project is determined by the actual allocation of manifested time we align with the established success criteria. When 100% of our essence is set to the task, you can rest assured that the work will be done in short order.

Common wisdom is aligned with the perspective that tomorrow is ethereal and yesterday is a memory. This baseline of perception brings us as earthly end-users to the fact that our focal point of strength is in the Now.

Allowing your thoughts to escape to the past and future leaks your lifeforce into the abyss. Corral your being to what is in right in front of you and you will reap the benefits of universal consciousness and the powerful abilities that come hand in hand with mindfulness.

Be your own governor of thought and reality, be the consciousness you can rely upon to ground you, and be well!

The Conscious Choice

The conscious choice we make in in our moment-to-moment experience to align our energy to our highest and best purpose is the grounding we create for happiness and fulfilment. This overt decision is what manifests our being and attunes it to the frequency that resonates in concordance with our life plan.

The path we walk is one that offers lessons and opportunity. The challenge we all face is maintaining the understanding that light always eclipses darkness when we allow the process to germinate and reach full bloom.

Situations will arise that appear on the surface to be a quick fix or a shorter path to the enlightenment we seek, when in reality these are tests of your resolve to maintain your course. There is no fast forward button to the goals we have in our mind's eye.

Know well that you are here to shine and this brilliance is your gift. This self-fulfilling prophecy is anchored in your heart center and the contract you have with the universe.

Be the being you have in your soul, be the precious commodity you know the world requires of you, and be well!

Compassion Leads to Connection

We always have a choice as to how we wish to perceive our environment. The surroundings we are ensconced within are open to our interpretation, and the alignment we choose sets the stage for the actions forthcoming.

The scope of our reality is based on our attunement to the light or the darkness we see in our fellows. The opportunity always exists to see either in any circumstance.

When we raise our frequency to the higher spectrum, we view the world through a lens that is pure of heart and connected to joy. Then, lower vibrations become white noise at best and do not affect our well-being or cheerful demeanor.

Know well that your life is yours to live in the fashion of your design. The path steeped in compassion leads to connection and camaraderie.

Be the light in your very being, be the conduit to kindness, and be well!

Soulful Expansion

The present moment in which we exist is the adventure we bring into being for our personal education and the betterment of the collective. This experience is uniquely encoded with our karmic DNA and tethered to the life plan we have set out to manifest into creation.

The mindful awareness we have of our ability to bring our visions to reality sets the stage and tempo for the interactions we encounter. This path is one that fills our heart and embodies our deepest beliefs and desires.

The acceptance of who we are allows for the continued metamorphosis towards the full realization of who we have always been. This journey has always been a chrysalis for our development on the Earth plain in alignment with the unmanifested heavenly domain.

Know well that your lessons are always custom designed for your soulful expansion and their benefits are universal in application. Your openness to what is, is the key to your progression, happiness and well-being.

Be 100% present in your life, be open to your growth and transcendence, and be well!

Authentically Our Own

The connection we have to our childhood is the north star we can always count on to guide us home. The realization that the truths that we held close to our hearts in our youth were, and still are, the baseline that we know to be authentically our own.

As youngsters, we were always aware of our surroundings and how the pieces all fit together on a larger universal scale. We may have not known the finer points that adults covet in the grown-up world, but we knew right from wrong, how to laugh and deeply love.

When we find the way back to where we came from, we elevate our consciousness to that place in the higher realm that cared for us with the gift of simplicity and joy. Know well that all you need is available to you for the asking because life provides through a symbiosis.

The give and take that governs our existence is on an honor system to be sure. The karmic wheel turns and the cosmic accountant is forever vigilant.

Trust in your path and find joy in what has always made sense to you in your core. You know all you need to know right now and what you don't is yours for the asking.

Be satisfied with your beginnings, be honored by the road you have traveled, and be well!

Ease of Passage

The life we set out to live is one of a joyful and fulfilling existence that we envision daily in our mind's eye. This path is the extension of our manifested dreams and the life plan we carry forward from our connection to the zero-point field.

This journey's grounding is based on the perceptions we create of our interactions and their outcomes. The cumulative effect of our experiences is the amalgamation of what we know in our hearts and what we perceive as our earthly needs and desires.

The key to experiencing a happy and tranquil life is simplicity. Mitigating confusion and complexity allows for an ease of passage so we may flourish.

Know well that we are here to learn in the format that best serves our higher purpose. Embrace what life offers with a calm understanding and an open heart.

Be content in yourself, be blissful in your simplicity, and be well!

Perspective is the Key

We arise from our slumber everyday with the opportunity to make a huge difference in our lives and the lives of others. The path we walk is one that leads to the destinations we choose through our interactions and the energetic frequency to which we align.

Some days are filled with sunshine and others with rain, but it's our outlook on our surroundings that emanates the vibrations that attract or repel others. Our perception is the determining factor for our existence on Earth.

Perspective is the key to joy and well-being. Knowing that no matter the circumstance, you can always set your personal view of the experience to be positive in nature that will allow you to find the happiness that is your birthright.

There is never a situation that is out of your control to create your own narrative for success. The criterion is yours and yours alone to decide what works best for you in the present moment.

Be Now in your mindset, be attuned to your inner goodness, and be well!

Our Own Self-Worth

The belief we have in our own self-worth is directly aligned to the acceptance of the life plan we have set out to achieve. This inner knowing is the correlation we work to manifest between doing and being.

The experiences we draw to us are the lessons we require to realize the goodness we have within our hearts. This essential understanding is the baseline for our presence on Earth and the opportunities we have to expand our ability to assist others on their journeys.

Through meditation, prayer and self-reflection, we create alignment with the collective. This deeper experience is one that heightens our awareness and allows mindfulness to flourish.

Be open to who you are, be in communication with your inner self, and be well!

Mindful Abstinence from Thought

The world in which we live is clearly intended as a training ground for our hopeful ascendence to the higher plains of reality. Like any form of exercise, the work we do on Earth is exhausting, and demands time to rest and recuperate.

Traditional thinking teaches us that sleep rejuvenates our bodies, and this truth is fundamentally correct in the manifested environment. What we are generally not taught is that our soul and its connection to the source also requires attention to operate at its peak performance.

The sort of focus that our upper chakras require is a mindful abstinence from thought. Time away from the thinking that creates the energy leaks into the past and future is what revitalizes our higher self.

When we open our minds to their fullest, we become one. This oneness allows us to draw from the cumulative base of energy and knowledge that feeds all things.

We have the tools at our fingertips to be at ease and empowered; training for this gift is as simple as being. Relax and look deeply inside yourself, and see all that you feel.

Be in restful action as you sense your connection to your surroundings, be your own master of well-being, and be well!

Heart Rhythms

The rhythms within our heart attune us to the surroundings in which we reside. This energetic flow is the balance we depend on to provide us our stability and connection.

Our heart-center contains earthly mooring points to time, space and all others known and unknown. This gateway within us is the conditional pathway to our upper consciousness.

Peace of mind is a manifested perception based on the reality we create. This conscious choice is always ours in conjunction with what we feel within and fathom as our universal understanding.

When alignment is created between our manifested environment and the acceptance of the external, we allow ourselves the foundational grounding we require. This personal baseline becomes our true north and always lights our way home.

Know well that you have the ability and the tools to build the shelter that suits your every need. This deeper realization is the simplified prerequisite for your well-being and happiness.

Be the construct of your design, be the light that shines bright, and be well!

Personal Power

Our energy is our personal power, and we have complete control of it as a precious resource. The focus we place on how we allocate our supply is the guiding principle of our time on Earth.

Like the rudder of a ship, our thoughts steer the vessel of our being. The manifested world is a front-end user interface for the universal power source that we are all blessed to be a part of as a working paradigm.

Know well that what you think is what you program, and what you program is what comes into being. The perception of your creation is the reality of your mind's eye.

Being mindful to elevate your consciousness above negativity like complaining and worry will reinforce the parameters you set to create a joyful experience. The world in which you live is by your design.

Be clear with your intention, be positive in your expression, and be well!

Be Patient with Yourself

The time and space in which we exist is intended for our growth and betterment. This hallowed ground is the blessing that we all have as our endowment.

The environment we inhabit is the playground we manifest for the education we call unto ourselves. Be patient with yourself in the classroom of your design.

The student is the archetype that we exist within on Earth. The moment-to-moment experience is the lesson plan created from your karmic blueprint.

The opportunity is eternally your own within the perceptions you embody. When you are open to what is presented, the silence you hold dear beckons the wisdom you seek.

Know well that your life is the gift you choose and joy is within you. Love and acceptance are the keys to unlocking the treasures in your mind's eye.

Be the patience you desire, be the catalyst of your own internal collaboration, and be well!

Journey of Mindfulness

Our lives are designed as an experience to maximize the opportunities that we manifest into creation. The task firmly lies upon us to build an existence for ourselves that beckons in the light and repels all else.

From the moment we arrived on Earth, we were gifted the ability to love and learn. The openness of our hearts connects us all to the source of deep knowledge and wisdom.

When we align our frequency to a channel that is well received by others in a common vibration, we enjoy a symbiosis of kindness and compassion. A shared journey of mindfulness is one that raises the collective consciousness.

Be grateful for your existence, be gracious with your time and energy, and be well!

Emotional Competency

We are all energetic beings subject to the vibratory experience of the environment in which we exist. The moment-to-moment interactions we participate in have the power to dictate the frequency to which we attune.

The knowledge that we are in control of our emotional competency is the cornerstone to stability. Taking an active role in your response to any situation is conscious living.

The ability to focus on positive functionality is what elevates us above the lower realm of consciousness into a mindful state. What awaits in the higher spaces is connection to the grander source.

Know well that when someone, something or some situation envelops you with negativity you can choose to not accept that gift as your own. You have the right to return to sender with no ill attached.

Next time you are at a park with a pond, you may have the opportunity to watch ducks going about their business; please pay close attention when two birds paddle too close to one another and a squabble ensues. As the birds separate from one another, they rear up in the water, flapping their wings, shaking off the negative vibration of the altercation as they move on with their day as if nothing ever happened.

We all will have the occasion to put this tool to use. It's up to us to look to nature for ways to mitigate unhealthy energy like fear, greed and anger.

Look inward and upward to the source of your being to light your path. The illumination is there as your guide and shines as bright as it's allowed.

Be above the disconnection, be a part of the solution, and be well!

Truth Resonates

The truth resonates in the highest of vibrations. Those who welcome the opportunity to share their thoughts and feelings in this hallowed ground are granted the deepest of connections that foster inner-peace and well-being.

Know well that the frequency that we align to on Earth is the governance of the path we travel, and this space becomes our blessing or our curse. The acceptance of this communication paradigm is key to tranquility.

When we learn to be at peace with what we know and how we share it with others, we open our being up to the vast possibilities of the universe. The removal of energetic blocks in your chakra system creates an internal synergy that manifests a symbiosis of trust between your soul and the collective.

Kindred spirits feel the need to build upon the goodwill that originally assembled the cohort. There are no barriers within the group, and knowledge becomes a tribal possession for all to bask in its clarity and understanding.

Be truthful in your interactions, be above reproach, and be well!

Eliminate the Breach

Our relationships are the connection and grounding that grants us perspective, energy and purpose. There is an innate need to be part of the tribe, even with all of the associated complications that arise from the dependencies that appear to be external to ourselves.

The knowledge that there is no disconnect between us and our fellows is a precept that governs the higher consciousness, but often eludes those who are resonating in the lower floors of perception. When our manifested experiences allow us to see beyond the earthly firewall, we accept the universal understanding of cosmic complexity.

The intricacy of the human condition is baffling, to say the least. The delicate pathways we all walk are mapped to what we believe to be personal goals, but in reality they are all overlapping in result and destination.

Transcendence becomes possible when we are able to see the world beyond the lens we think we know and open our mind to the vast possibilities that quell the confusion. We are all working toward the same goal: happiness.

The ability to open your heart to others eliminates the breach and fills it in with understanding and compassion. Know well that there is no need to overthink, overreact or overcompensate.

Be real to others, be true to yourself, and be well!

Our Desired Presentation

The emanation of our vibrations is ours to create. The opportunity is omnipresent to align our perspective with our desired presentation to the world.

Know well there is always a conscious choice to be made, and we own that gift. The tools are at your fingertips to select the hallowed space you wish to inhabit.

Visualize the manifested environment as a 12-story building with an elevator at your ready. The bank of buttons that lay before you allow you passage to the vibratory frequency in your mind's eye.

The inhabitants of the floors that align with your choosing are the cohort of your manifestation. These fellow travelers will support your endeavors with the lessons you require.

The construct is yours to design. The architecture, the denizens and the surroundings all mirror your thoughts and desires.

Be the master of your domain, be the creator of goodness, and be well!

Frequency of Accomplishment

We all are here to accomplish the goals we have in our mind's eye. The knowledge that our existence is purposeful is the hallmark of mental and physical well-being.

The tasks we have on our to-do lists are by design the framework that is created to support our internal infrastructure. The wireframe we construct and maintain is both for our stability and connection to our surroundings.

As we review what we have on our plate to achieve, we must always acknowledge our own ability and desire to do our best work; the secret sauce is simply caring. Knowing that you have the tools, desire and connection to do the needful is the key to getting the ball rolling on even most daunting of projects.

This positive state of mind attunes your frequency to that of accomplishment, and this vibration will beckon to you all you need to be successful. Rest assured that the path you manifest is the one you have mapped in conjunction with your higher purpose.

Be brave, be resolute in your focus, and be well!

Your School of Life

We all come into this world with a deep connection, memory and understanding of the unmanifested realm from which we just emerged. This birthright is one that is fostered by some and allowed to fade into atrophy by others.

By nurturing our inner self, we maintain what we have always known. This inner child we all possess at the core is the very essence of our being.

Creativity, compassion, kindness and the ability to connect without fear of judgment or disparagement is at the root of our soul's knowledge base. When we elevate our consciousness to allow our true selves to reign over our earthly interactions, we find that purity and truth become the overarching theme.

Our time on this planet is intended for education and growth. Life is a cosmic university where the only entrance criteria is birth and graduation is guaranteed with the degree of your effort and choosing.

Survival is paramount to the earthbound traveler, but experience is essential to the advancement of the soul. Know profoundly that your work here has deep purpose and that your syllabus is clear to you as the eternal student.

Be your higher self's high cover, be the dean of your school of life, and be well!

Cosmic Soundtrack

We all have a personal agenda we set out to fulfill every day. Our tasks range in their scope and influence.

The perspective we have on our plans is one that we hold dear, as it is created from an individualistic success criterion. This universal axiom of truth is a guiding principle we can all rely on to shed light onto our being.

If we step back and allow ourselves to elevate our consciousness to a higher place where we can look down on our cohort, we see a picture that sheds light on connective tissue that joins us all energetically. These unmanifested fibers of light are the interwoven threads that bind the universal purpose of being.

When we become one with our natural state, we accept that there is truly only one conductor for the symphony we all hear. The cosmic soundtrack, if you listen closely, grants you insights into the deepest of thoughts and desires of the others around you, and this gift grants the harmonic understanding that is compassion and empathy.

Be in tune with what you hear, be the first chair player of your life, and be well!

Denizens of the Universe

As denizens of the universe, we all have certain unalienable rights and abilities bestowed upon us. These gifts range in magnitude, depending on your alignment with your life purpose and the frequency to which you attune.

The opportunity is always there for you to channel the cosmic source's energy to the focus of your desire. The present moment opens this portal as the gateway to unbridled power and knowledge.

As human beings, we are generally granted the five basic senses of sight, hearing, smell, taste and touch. These manifested receivers all work in conjunction with each other to maximize the grounding in our surroundings.

One of many conduits to the higher realm exists when we bypass earthly inputs. Shutting down what we have accepted as reality in the third dimension and fostering what our deeper being knows transports us to the unmanifested space.

The view from the penthouse of our experience is not one we see, hear, smell, touch or taste. It is one that envelops us in the warmth and connection to the heavens.

Let go, close your eyes, let the force you feel within you be your guiding light. The mastery you require is always yours to invoke as a birthright.

Be fearless, be the composer of your own works of art, and be well!

More Than Meets the Eye

Our relationships are the cornerstone of our well-being. The connections we create are the conduits we rely on for energetic interaction.

We walk the Earth within the vessel of our birth with daily offerings to enhance our experiences. The opportunity to commune with fellow travelers is the omnipresent gift that life offers.

The frequency you have attuned your vibration to will open you to receive as you desire. Every passerby is a beacon of light that may illuminate your being if given the chance.

Hold no preconceived notions based on what you believe you know. There is always more than meets the eye.

Be gregarious in your space, be a karmic ambassador of goodwill, and be well!

Along the Way

Life is a challenge to be met with open arms, as you came here with a purpose in your mind's eye. A positive perspective is the key to your achieving the goals you set for yourself upon entry.

The preloaded factory-installed features you came with and the lessons learned along the way are what make you a unique masterpiece to behold. The ability to laugh at life situations, and most importantly, yourself, is what allows you the freedom to live knowing you possess the clarity of mind and stability of soul to weather any storm.

There are no shoulds, no I wish I hads, and no regrets that are worthy of lowering your self-image. Life is here for you to enjoy in the beauty and power of the present moment while learning, growing and laughing along the way.

Be kind and courteous to all you meet, be an ambassador for contentment, and be well!

Acceptance, Compassion and Connection

Life on Earth is intentionally designed to be a challenge. We come here to work on acceptance, compassion and connection. Many of the lessons we seek may not always present themselves clearly to us at first glance.

As we venture onward, the teachings we require will reoccur on our path, gaining power in their effects as they recycle. As we elevate our consciousness, we learn to accept the what is without the need to question the why is.

Taking this leap of faith is the linkage of our earthly presence with heavenly spirit. The transcendence of our awareness is the creation of our escalated being.

This higher space is the hallowed experience that breathes wind into our manifested lungs and infinite reality into the zero-point field of the universe. Trust what you feel as the anchor of your perception, as the soul knows your path and is only limited by your mind.

Be mindful of your need to accept, be at peace with your knowledge of what is, and be well!

Inward Affection

The energy that radiates from our manifested being is the aligning factor for the frequency of our very existence. When we make the conscious effort to smile, we raise our vibration to the highest spectrum available to us.

The knowledge that we possess this tool grants us complete mastery of our demeanor. When we shed light on ourselves, we illuminate our perception and the environment around us.

As we sit in private mediation or in a crowded room, our auric field radiates the energy we bring into being. Know well that your self-care always ranks first and foremost, and that loving kindness is best received internally when the expression on your face lights up the room with a heartfelt smile.

Be the recipient of your inward affection, be the companion in your life, and be well!

Profound Meaning

Our lives have profound meaning, and that purpose is ours for the making. As we look around, we see the reality of our perception.

The knowledge that as we journey in this manifested space, we have the option to maintain control of our emotions and our reactions affords us peace of mind. Staying in the higher spaces grants freedom from fear and mitigates the exposure to others rooting in the darkness.

Your experience is truly what you make it; look within for the instruments you have created to pilot the expedition. You need no guide other than your imagination to build the life of your intentions.

Be powerful within your realizations, be cognizant of your capabilities, and be well!

The Universal Coefficient

All it takes to raise your vibration and that of those around you is to smile. The frequency we attune to when our emotions are in a state of bliss is one and the same with pure loving energy.

As we radiate joy, we raise the state of consciousness for the others in our proximity. The light we embody is a beacon for others to follow the trail you blazed to this enlightened perspective.

Look no farther than your own outlook on life to enhance the universal coefficient for kindness, compassion and caring. You are as powerful as you choose to allow yourself to be in life.

Be a light worker, be one who serves, and be well!

Joy Comes From Within

Our lives have been a parade of experiences, all manifesting themselves into ideals and perceptions. These perceived values shape our outward facing persona and become the vehicle that carries us through our earthbound travels.

The joy we find comes from within. This internal sanctuary is the garden in which we sit to grasp the meaning of what we seek.

The lessons we have learned on our journey have all had purpose as they have exposed our consciousness to the grander picture we are intended to see. These travels have been focused on the execution of the plan that nurtures our core beliefs and feeds our soul's purpose for being.

The inner space that we hold dear illuminates the path we walk and the vibration we emanate. Know well that the security we all strive to achieve is nestled safely within our essence.

The castle walls we have built to protect our well-being are in reality a hinderance to peace of mind. Their construct limits our ability to see the beauty all around us.

Be aligned with your inner knowledge, be the blossoming that opens your soul to what truly is your meaning, and be well!

Building Your Environment

The emotions we perceive as our state of being align to the vibrations we radiate. This manifestation presents itself as the essence of our speech and body language.

As we attune to the frequency of our perception, we make the overt decision to adapt our consciousness to the corresponding level of enlightenment. Know well that you welcome and/or repel others in this manner of engagement.

There is a universal scale that affixes the spirit of what we feel with its equivalent space in the cosmos. Higher level sentiments like joy, peace, gratitude and love are the hallowed ideals that open the doors to prosperity, while the negative energy surrounding anger, complaining and deceit are the dense low vibrations that hold you back and weigh you down in karmic bankruptcy.

Making the conscious effort to be mindful of your thoughts, words and actions assures your control of your domain. Look no farther than the mirror to know who's in charge of your own destiny.

Be grateful for your awareness, be an active participant in building your environment, and be well!

What Shapes Our Being

The quality of our lives is determined by the internal barometer we set. The success criteria we employ for our happiness is of our own design.

The vibrations we emanate are in alignment with the frequency to which we attune. The experience we beckon to us is the prevailing theme in the realm of our creation.

The fellow travelers we attract into our space shape our being. The energy these kindred spirits share guides our passage.

Know well that your life's lessons are constructed to bring you a wealth of knowledge and well-being. The acceptance that the road will not always be a simple one is the key to a safe journey.

Contentment is found in our peace of mind, and this joy is welcomed home to us through connection. The knowing that we are not alone on our quest is the bridge to the deeper being that softens the path we must walk on Earth.

Be in alignment with your own presence of perception, be the manifested magnificence that resides in your soul, and be well!

Circumstance and Action

Our lives are best lived in concert with our surroundings. When we are open to what comes our way, we flow and flourish.

There is never a qualified requirement for friction, as harmony is best served when circumstance and action are aligned with our higher purpose. Know well that our goals and the path we walk are not contained within a vacuum.

The acceptance that our vision is one of millions of variables that align to manifest the world in which we are blessed to create brings with it health and happiness. A freeform lifestyle is one that welcomes change and growth with open arms and a blissful mindset.

Be attuned to the needs and wishes of others, be flexible in your response and availability, and be well!

Enter Zen Here

The experiences we all have within our days are intended as portals to a deeper understanding of our journey's meaning. The opportunity is always ours to attune our consciousness to the higher frequency that connects us to universal knowledge and well-being.

The entry point to zen is no farther than your breath. When we clear our minds of earthly chatter, we become the doorway that is always there for our passage.

As we venture to walk through this opening, we find the hallowed ground that resides within us all as we step out of what we thought we knew into what we feel in union with the higher realm of reality. The amplification of cosmic time and space resonates within our core as we create a connection with our highest purpose and settle into what guides our being.

The path is always there for our manifestation. Follow your spirit as it knows the way home.

Be the acceptance that resides at your core, be the calm in your knowing, and be well!

Light Verses Darkness

The experiences that we are blessed with present us the opportunity to create the fluid life blueprint we have in our mind's eye. The perception we embrace sets the frequency we attune to as the baseline for our personal reality.

The choice is yours to live in darkness or light. There is immediate gratification from both selections, but long-term growth and joy is only fostered in the goodness of the light.

As plants naturally turn to the sun for their photosynthetic stimulation, human beings require the warmth and kindness that is only found in the higher space of universal connection. The upper realm sees no fear, disconnection or discourse; here there is clarity of mind and purpose.

Love is the highest of all vibrations, and its resonation purifies our very being. Alignment with the source of creation boosts your personal frequency and beckons like-minded others into your world.

Be mindful that your choices determine your ultimate destination, be an active participant in your life's mapping, and be well!

Our Conscious Cohort

The tribe we create is an amalgamation of who we know as our biological family and the souls we are blessed to welcome into our hearts and cross our paths along the way. This conscious cohort is the masterpiece of the energetic manifestation of our purpose on Earth.

We call to us the situations that work to our highest and best purpose. The players involved in our growth lessons come to us for our acceptance as we perceive them as friend or foe. When we allow our experiences to shape our learning patterns, we open ourselves up to the full scope of understanding that we are intended to absorb.

The knowledge that every moment is a precious opportunity is the working paradigm that springboards us to the higher realms of consciousness. Know in your heart that you possess the ability to form the alliances you require to be successful in all aspects of your life.

Our journey comes with no physical map or instruction guide; when we allow presence to be our teacher, we see all we require. When accepted fully, this axiom is universal in application and nurtures our well-being on every level.

Be in alignment with those in your space, be open to receive the alms they contribute to the joint effort, and be well!

What You Think You See

Have you looked around you today? I mean truly looked past what you think you see and experienced the essence of the space you inhabit?

The world in which we live is heaven on Earth. The perception of our vision is what manifests into our reality.

When we step back from the daily inputs we have allowed to govern our thought process, we gift ourselves the magic as it is intended to be received. This playground contains all we could ever desire and it's available to us on demand.

The joy is literally in the air when your lungs are primed with the kindness and compassion that is required to fathom the depths of the beauty we have been endowed with on this plain of existence. Please know this in your heart.

Be the watcher of what you know to be true, be the kindness that holds the door ajar for others to follow you home, and be well!

Artistry of Our Design

The world we live in is the projection of our perception and its effects on our collective connection with the universal source. The manifestation of our beliefs is the artistry of our design.

Our dreams put into action become the medium by which the canvas of our existence springs to life. The broad brush strokes our experiences create become the backdrops that are fine-tuned by a steady hand guiding the intricacies that make us unique.

The opportunity to express your feelings and desires as a world vision is the platform from which your exalted-self reigns true. Embrace your core values as the imagery that will shape creation.

Be overt in your expression, be the color that brings imagination to life, and be well!

Outstretched Arms

The deep connection we seek in life is found through the outstretched arms of friendship and camaraderie. The bonds we create with our fellows opens the pathways to the higher consciousness that resonates on the frequency of loving kindness.

As we work to build the existence we see in our mind's eye, we come to the understanding that nothing meaningful is ever created in a vacuum. This knowing opens our being to the expansive resources the universe has to offer.

When we align our energetic essence to the collective, we maximize the opportunity we have to expand our bandwidth to draw from the source. The pipeline is infinite and our ability to receive is unbridled.

Cherish those who you beckon to your side. They are the gift that amplifies our spirit and illuminates our path.

Be the creator of karmic goodwill, be open to the love as its returned to you, and be well!

Opportunity and Potential

We all subscribe to a program of sorts on one level or another to guide our path and create an infrastructure that builds toward the success criteria of our design. The deeper we allow these roots to dwell, the grander the possibilities for our soul's expansion.

The source of the universal energetic experience derives its essence from the collective. The choice is ours and ours alone as to what level we wish to tap into the shared mainline for its life sustaining power.

Every frequency has its own opportunity and potential. As we walk through the days of our creation, we pilot our vessel in accordance with the vibration we manifest.

The will of our making is what we share with our fellow travelers. This outward expression of our inner being is the soul's truest source in connection and creation.

Letting go opens the road to the fulfillment in your mind's eye. Knowing with the highest confidence that your very being is safe and will be sanctified is the prize for those ready and willing to be at peace with it all.

Be true to your being in its highest form, be in concordance with life, and be well!

Means of Communication

The essence of our being is projected to the world in which we live through the means of communication we employ. The words we share are a powerful connective tool.

These pearls we string together verbally or in written from are an outreach from our soul to kindred spirits. We are truly blessed to share a vibratory alignment with those open to receive the message we send.

Know in your heart that our ability to connect is not limited to one means. A simple kind look, smile or hugs says much.

The path we walk is one that interconnects us to our fellow travelers. Our ability to create a symbiosis is what raises the collective spirit.

When we come to the realization that our journey is but one of many threads of the same reality, we truly begin our transcended experience. The openness to building bridges through intention and interaction is what elevates joint consciousness.

Be the synapse that conjoins kindness from Heaven to Earth, be the understanding that illuminates the way, and be well!

Mindful Construction

Inside us all is a portal that connects us to the source of all creativity, kindness and understanding. Our soul is the union of our earthly manifested traits with all those capabilities we have access to in the unmanifested realm.

As we elevate our consciousness, we unlock the doors that previously appeared unpassable. The knowledge that our awareness is the key to what seemed beyond our scope is all the grounding we need to create infinite possibilities.

When we apply the very essence of our being to our path, we illuminate our steps with hallowed energy. The opportunity to add love to our incantation raises the vibration to an unmatched level of existence in this realm.

The soul we create on our journey is not ours alone. The mindful construction we establish is a link to karmic completion.

Be aware of your inner gifts, be open to sharing your power, and be well!

Collective Mission

The world in which we live was created to shelter and nurture us as individuals working on a collective mission. The goal at hand is the growth and betterment of the whole.

The knowledge that we are all connected at the core is the depth that bonds life as we know it to a universal consciousness. As awareness grows, we align with the plentiful bounty that awaits us all.

Safety, security and happiness is the gift that is our birthright. Omnipotence lies just beneath the surface for our senses to perceive.

When we remove the barriers, we feel the love and connection that is always there for our benefit. An open heart is all that is required for your eternal well-being.

Be blissfully linked through kindness and compassion, be the reality of the energetic expansiveness, and be well!

Heaven as a State of Being

Our expedition on Earth is a generally viewed as the stepping stone or stopgap before we reach our final cosmic destination. This perspective, while prevalent in the middle frequencies, is limiting in its very nature.

The journey we all travel in the manifested realm is aligned with the intentions we set and the lens we use as our optics. The knowledge that the environment in which we reside is of our making is the key to a blissful existence.

Heaven is not a place, nor is it a destination; it is our state of being. The attunement to our chosen vibration sets the coordinates for where we transport our very essence.

Death is not an end, but in reality a portal to the next phase of our consciousness. Raising our awareness above the fear of what we experience on Earth is the passport to the higher realm.

Know well that you have the capability to establish daily residence in the kingdom of heaven. The coordinates are yours to unlock with the solutions of your design.

Be karmically composed, be steadfast in your connection, and be well!

Visions of Beauty

The connection we have with our surroundings is a feeling that emanates from our sense of belonging. This inner knowing is the bond we have with our life purpose and the frequency to which we align our earthly vibratory experience.

The visions of beauty that we manifest in our mind's eye are an extension of our personal reality. This state of being is what we refer to as consciousness.

Our awareness of perception is the mindfulness that creates our persona and its corresponding alignment with the grander source. This sense of deeper being transcends the manifested world and conjoins our essence with the collective.

Know in your heart that your visions of beauty are akin to that of others in your similar space. You are never alone in your ability to draw peace and tranquility from the upper realm when you allow your heart to remain open and thoughts free of fear.

Be true to your own knowing, be compassion at your core, and be well!

Loving Energy

The way we choose to live our lives is a gift that we present to ourselves. The opportunity to immerse our very being in loving energy is the foundation for health, happiness and well-being.

The law of attraction is a cornerstone of the universal infrastructure. This knowledge grants us one of many tools to live in the light.

When the focus of our existence is in a space where love is at the core of our intentions, our vibrations attune to the very source. The alchemy we create manifests positivity and joy into existence.

Know well that the frequency assigned to the vibration of love is the highest of all possible earthly spaces. The view from this platform is pure magnificence to behold.

Be your own prerequisite for serenity, be comfortable in your calm, and be well!

Positive Expression

The window of our perception is the lens by which we view the world we create. The knowledge that our imagery is the foundation of our experience is the tethering point we can count on for stability and grounding.

The visions in our mind's eye become the blueprint we use in the manifestation of our earthly resonance. The frequency we align to in this endeavor sets us on the path of our choosing.

There is freedom in our choices and compassion in our hearts as we enjoy the adventure we beckon to us. This journey is of our free will and its joy our responsibility.

Know well that you are the purveyor of your personal destiny. Live this life to its fullest with the awareness you are connected through mindfulness and love.

Be positive in your expression, be the power and faith behind your intentions, and be well!

Sacred Mission

The search for the answers to life's deepest questions is truly not the holy grail we quest for; the energy expended in this vein is a distraction at best. There is no sparkly object that fills the void that you may feel in your heart.

The schism you may be enduring in your soul is a self-inflicted wound that is simply rectified though your own loving kindness and personal nurture. The cultivation of a self-awareness practice is the first step in filling in the missing pieces.

The acceptance that your reason for being is as unique as your very DNA allows you to embrace your birthright as a traveler on a sacred mission. The journey will follow no map and has no preordained end point; what it does have and guarantees is growth of mind and spirit.

Your waking moments define the day's path, and this window is to be seized without fail and used to its fullest magical extent. Your intentions in this hallowed space will be heard and the tracks will be laid to the stations that await.

Look no farther than yourself for the why in your life. Your prospectus is artwork in progress and the timeline is infinitely yours for the creation.

Be open to what happens, be righteous in your commitment to your path, and be well!

As We Mature

Life is our ever-present challenge to create and maintain our personal freedom through connection, consciousness and compassion. This journey is one that starts within us as we strive to comprehend the grander meaning and our ability to serve.

As we mature, we gain an understanding that our purpose has an inward focus, but its power is derived from the collective. This awakening spawns our ability to draw energy from the source and utilize its power to manifest the visions of joy we have for ourselves and the others we hold close.

The knowing we embrace becomes our truth, and this true north our guide. Simply being nurtures the inward light we shine to illuminate our way and a beacon for kindred spirits to recognize as needed.

Be true to your heart, be accepting of others, and be well!

Societal Success Criteria

The quality of the feelings we have for others is deeply dependent upon the choices we make in regards to our own resonant vibration. The frequency we attune to aligns us to others in a similar space.

The knowledge that our own free will is the catalyst for connection is an extremely powerful tool. The ability to share our loving kindness with kindred spirits is a blessing that elevates the collective.

The universal energetic experience is an ongoing manifestation that ebbs and flows along with the communal consciousness. As our species heightens awareness, we increase the baseline for perception.

Know well that your aptitude for goodness plays a huge part in the societal success criteria. Embracing the construct that maintains the karmic infrastructure allows for individual contributors to convert their personal intentions into global amendments.

Be an ambassador for kindheartedness, be an empathetic soul, and be well!

Sincere Knowing

At the core of our very being is the sincere knowing that we are the essence of pure love. This deep alignment to the universal source of connection, creativity and compassion is what guides and protects us.

We are, and will always remain the focal point of our energetic experience. This rooting in self is the pathway to the vast power that life has to offer.

Through our earthly cohort, we build a network of like-minded souls who share in our resonate vibration. This alignment of frequency boosts our energy and enhances our ability to see our loving likeness in the world around us.

The process is cyclical and the personal experience becomes a bidirectional exchange of energy between the Heaven and Earth. This be told, our only prerequisite to maintain the cycle is a pure heart and loving soul.

Be the manifestation of your own desired self-worth, be the love that envelops the world, and be well!

Minimize Overthinking

Energy moves like water, and our thoughts coexist in a symbiosis with this flow. The ability to regulate our thinking patterns is a skill to be mastered to ensure throughput and a consistency of design.

The personal infrastructure we manifest creates an internal information highway for our downloaded data from on high to mingle with the perceptions we align to in the earthly space.

This balance is the alchemy that stabilizes our perspective with our bandwidth's capabilities to receive. Positive thoughts have an extremely light footprint, while negativity is a heavy payload.

It is our most ardent responsibility to manage our superstructure in such a way that we maximize possibilities and minimize unnecessary overthinking. Know well that remaining in a present state of mind will act as the governor you require to filter out the unwanted flotsam and jetsam.

The Now contains all you need to ensure stability, positivity and a cohesive state of mind. Focus your being in presence and you will be at home in your essence.

Be fluid by design, be mindful 24/7, and be well!

Your Inner Smile

Our days are intended to fulfill our soul's purpose, enlighten our consciousness and bring joy to our hearts. With this as our mission statement we walk the Earth knowing wholeheartedly that our connection to our fellows stimulates growth and prosperity.

When we gift ourselves the ability to elevate our vibration to a state of happiness, we attract others on that same frequency. As we continue to amass a cadre of mindful travels we see the collective view that is only available to those in the higher space.

This unobstructed picturesque landscape becomes home for mind and spirit. The essence of our being is truly captivated when the contentment that we all seek is allowed to shine brightly.

The search for serenity need not elude you. Look no farther than your inner smile to brighten your days.

Be the spark that ignites the fire that burns within you, be that which brings elation to your life, and be well!

Cosmic Accounting

Our hearts are open vessels that connect us energetically. The magic of the universe is governed within us from this portal.

We are the masters of our own karma and the practices we put into action. The knowledge that the cosmos works in an orderly fashion guarantees consistency of response.

As we work to fulfill our calling to share our wealth of understanding and kindness, it becomes apparent that our surplus of goodness manifests a boomerang effect. The raised vibrations that are the byproduct of our outreach stimulates a symbiosis that in turn fills our hearts with warmth and joy.

The more you contribute to the common good, the more dividends you receive. The cosmic accounting is a simple debit and credit system.

Know well that your compassion is earmarked to your personal account and in parallel, reported in the general ledger we all share as a species. This redundancy is the wind in the sails that moves us forward as a collective.

Be giving of your time and goodwill, be a caretaker for those in need, and be well!

We are Here to Serve

Our personal meaning of life is the mystery that we all search for in our daily existence. Please know that the answer is as simple as we choose it be.

The knowledge that there is something bigger than our individual essence is the first step in the deepest of understandings. The acknowledgment that our connection to what we perceive as self finds its way through our connection to others.

The path to happiness is built through an awareness that we are here to serve. The joy we find in life comes when we foster the advancement of our fellows' needs and best wishes.

There is nothing more uplifting than creating a smile on another's face. This shared resonance is the springboard for your elevation to a mindful frequency attunement.

Be the joy in the air, be a mile marker on other's path to find the collective consciousness, and be well!

An Active State of Awe

Our intentions are the tools we use to shape our perception and its consequent reality. The artistry we are capable of has no limitations beyond our own dimension.

As we open our energetic observation to the vastness of possibility, we awaken the arteries that allow the life blood of the universe to flow. The cosmic condition draws its sustenance from the source we are all in attunement with at our deepest level of conscience.

The opportunity to utilize spirit to manifest your internal vision of self into an external creation is a gift well deserved. Know that your best self is only one action beyond your mind's eye.

You are Heaven on Earth. The acceptance of this hallowed condition is all one requires to transcend all preconceived boundaries.

Be in an active state of awe with your very being, be the architect of your own superstructure, and be well!

Both Heaven and Earth

There is an inner knowing we all have within us that grounds us in the reality we create and hold dear. This knowing is the faith we lean on that becomes the stability in our life.

As we journey onward through our adventures, we realize that our perspective is the creative energy that paints perception. The imagery that we manifest is based on the knowledge we have amassed from our life experiences.

At our core, we have a connection to our deeper purpose, and this sense of being is what anchors our path and guides our soul. Every step we take is one that sees us gain ground toward the next milestone on our personal road to accomplishment.

The baseline we use as a litmus test for success is tethered to both Heaven and Earth. The challenge we face is living in both domains as our understanding deepens and our connection becomes steadfast.

Be an energetic conductor, be the curator of your own collection of masterpieces, and be well!

Mission Control

There are many schools of thought on what the criteria is as far as setting the stage for our earthly engagement. Know in your heart that we all play a huge role in the pre-game planning for our lives.

Life is a balance of what we came here to learn, juxtaposed with what we have the ability to share. The unmanifested realm acts as the launch site and mission control for the big show that connects our soul with an earthbound experience.

Part of our preparation is choosing not only our parents, but the core tenants that make up our projected path for the trails to come. There is a powerful symbiosis between ourselves and the mothers and fathers of our selection.

The knowledge that you have been an active participant in the process affords you absolute ownership of all nine innings and any extras that you have gifted yourself. We have all literally signed up for the ride of our lives.

Know well that you always have the ability to adjust and fine tune your preparation through ongoing reinforcements and energic augmentations. Your parents are not limited to the ones that birthed you; our family is not restricted to blood relations, as we meet much of our kin along the way.

Be mindful, accepting and loving of who you choose to guide and govern the parameters of your youth, be in alignment with your overarching vantage point, and be well!

No Stone Goes Unturned

The daily mission we find ourselves on is one that stems from our intrinsic motivation to better ourselves and our life situation. No stone goes unturned as we look for the teachers, careers and material objects that enhance our station in life.

As we look beyond ourselves for the connection our quest requires, we generally overlook the simple fact that all we need is at our fingertips. The teachings we thirst for are always within the realm of our creation.

The knowing that the lesson plan is always ours to manifest leads us back to the mirror to see the person who holds the keys to success and enlightenment. There is no champion better suited than one's self as the tale is told and the deeds are done.

Be the action of your own design, be the advocate for your cause, and be well!

Pack Lightly

We all are in actuality intertwined souls contained within earthbound vessels. These cosmic capsules house our essence as it relates to matters here in the manifested realm.

The choice is ours as to what level of attunement we elect to vibrate our perception. As we climb the ladder of understanding toward the higher spaces, we gain the acceptance that our bandwidth is as burstable as we need it to be.

Our capacity to consume is infinite in the upper bands and more constrained in the lower floors of existence. The scope of our volume is in direct correlation to the density of the matters to which we are involved.

Please know that the lower the vibration of the issues in your preview, the more space it requires for storage. Drama is an energy hog, while love and kindness are ethereal on the storage scale.

The key technique to living your life in a calm and fluid way is to maintain a manageable load. Pack lightly and only carry your own bags, knowing well that you have reserved capacity for overflow when seasonally required.

Be radiant in your sphere of influence, be aware of your impact on others in your environment, and be well!

Self-Propelling Processes

We are the Alpha and Omega of our own existence. This inner connection we have to self is the conduit we maintain to the energetic source.

Through our love and compassion of self, we align our being with the grand scheme of the universe. The presence we have in our ability to share our essence with others is the bond by which we align with the cosmos.

Know well that you are your own sanctuary, and this inner shrine to well-being is the core energy that you build from to power the resources of your life. The self-propelling processes we create are based on our own inner strength in connection with our master plan's alignment with the greater good.

Be kind to yourself, be compassionate to others, and be well!

Higher State of Awareness

As we relax, we open our senses to their fullest capacity to receive. When we are in a state of enjoyment, our attunement is aligned to a channel that welcomes positive energy, and the outcomes we would expect in a higher state of awareness.

The Now brings with it the ultimate in focus and ability to achieve. The acceptance that you are where you need to be and that you are doing what you must facilitates the universe's energetic follow and guarantees success.

The truth of the matter is that the vibration we emanate is ours to consciously govern. The perception of our environment is of our making, and this state of creation is our self-manifested Heaven or Hell.

Raising yourself above the stress and concerns will provide you with the vantage point you require to assess your best options. Know you have complete control of the sensory inputs that regulate your physical and emotional well-being.

Be a catalyst for calm, be committed to positive creation, and be well!

Purposeful Being

The energetic output we manifest in connection with our surroundings is received by the outward world as our epitaph. The footprint we create through our intentions and interactions is one that blazes our trails and sets our standards for purposeful being.

The words we use are the most overt of our interactive tools. The power of our utterances should be held in the highest of reverence.

Know well that your connection to others is at the core of your well-being, and that your communication is the at the forefront of your ability to manage and maintain your precious relationships. Using your words to create symbiosis in mind and spirit will elevate individual and collective consciousness.

Be the one to recognize the magic in your presence, be the Now in your essence, and be well!

Directional Harmony

We all have a purpose to fulfill here on Earth. The journey for many of us is to determine our life's calling, and for some it is as clear as day.

As the adventure unfolds for those seeking a destination, the puzzle pieces begin to fit together as our level of acceptance aligns with presence. The joy we derive draws its power from the Now.

The resonance achieved in the present moment connects those on their karmic pilgrimage with those in a state of directional harmony. The collaborative energies raise the cumulative vibration and elevate the grander environment for all to enjoy the positive benefits.

Know well that our existence is a pixel in the universal portrait. This work of art is the masterpiece that brings love, laughter and contentment to the world.

Be accepting of the gratification in your life, be peaceful in your existence, and be well!

Adjust as Your Soul Requires

We are born with a mission in our mind's eye. The knowledge of what we set out to manifest in our earthly incarnation is one that plans to fulfill our growth needs and deepen our connection to spirit.

As we work through the trials and tribulations life offers, we may find that our goals change based on the lessons we learn. The experiences we are blessed with open our eyes and expand our perspective.

The vision we had for our lives is one that sets the stage for our encounters and its resonance is the overarching theme that holds us on our general course. The acceptance that we ebb and flow with the tides of our time is what allows us to flourish and become the who we ultimately intend to be.

Know in your heart that you will always accomplish your goals. Grant yourself the latitude to adjust as your soul requires.

Be flexible with your resolve, be supportive of your deeper knowing, and be well!

Unencumbered Access

The energy we reserve for ourselves comes from a deep well at the universe's core. This source of inspiration that powers our soul may feel as if it's our personal cache, when in reality, it truly manifests from the karmic reservoir.

The connection we maintain with the high space allows for unencumbered access to a free flow of knowledge, courage and kindness. With an open heart, we are able to bridge the gaps between individual concerns and external pressures.

The empathy we create for our fellow travelers illuminates the way and raises the vibration to a resonance aligned to a higher frequency. The knowledge that there is no energetic disconnect between us and our cohorts grants us the reprieve from fear to welcome in the creativity that may have been stifled in the lower realms.

Know well that you are as autonomous as you choose to be and your autonomy is part of the grander scheme that unites us all. The understanding we maintain of an omnipresent energy is the white light that shrouds us all in potential prosperity.

Be yourself, be connected, and be well!

Powerful Pause

We must always cherish the fact that we are our own inner sanctum. There is never any question that within us is the strength and courage to protect our essence and guide our soul's connection to the light.

Know in your heart that your physical manifestation is a vessel for your deeper being. This container is well equipped with all of the safety mechanisms you require to maintain connection to the higher realm.

Look no farther than your breath to calm and ground you. This light within you controls focus, mindfulness and inner peace.

Redirect your attention to your inhalation and exhalation through the expansion and contraction of your lungs and chest. Look deep within this life-sustaining process to bridge the gap between Heaven and Earth.

The acceptance that we are here to learn is the knowing that illuminates the classroom of your life's existence. There is always the opportunity for a karmic time out and you are free to summon this powerful pause as your heart desires.

Be kind to yourself, be mindful of your capacity, and be well!

Fluidity

No matter where we are in our life cycle as a human being, we can rest assured that we are exactly where we are meant to be. This grounding knowledge is all it takes to focus on what matters most: our own happiness and well-being.

Learning to let go of over-thinking is a skill that requires Herculean efforts to master. The ability to be in the present moment, dusting off the residue of the past and maintaining your focus on presence, is the space to be cherished.

There is a natural flow to life, a karmic river that we all are immersed in on Earth. The decision is ours as to what extent we grant ourselves the gift to ride the energetic wave patterns as they come, or protest what is by swimming upstream.

Having faith in yourself will allow fluidity with the powers that be to shelter and guide your progression. Trusting the universe to protect your best interest is the acceptance that opens the doors to the grandeur of your own manifestation.

Be aligned with your willingness to release the past, be in the Now, and be well!

Rooted in Our Soul

The opportunity we have to live a full and happy life is a gift that is granted to us through the perspective we choose. The knowing that we are only truly alive in the present moment is the amplification of the universal wisdom at our disposal.

As we venture to fulfill the passions that suit our needs and aspirations, we come to realize that our master plan is always in play in the background of our daily lives. This omnipresent, stored procedure rooted in our soul is the connection we all maintain to the back end of the zero point field's heavenly energy.

When we let go of the outcomes that tie us to an earthly existence, we transcend the state of self and elevate our being to the grander scale. Know well that you are on course, and all roads lead to the beauty that is in store for your highest and best purpose.

Be above the linear, be the continuation of your mind's eye, and be well!

Light Workers

Our deepest connection to spirit is through our openness to the kindred souls in our lives. These angels who walk amongst us are the light workers we rely on to illuminate our way.

The friends and family we are blessed with are our earthly grounding as well as a conduit to the heavens. Know well that while we lean on others for support, we simultaneously are providing comfort and guidance to those in our queue to support on their journey.

The groups to which we belong are assembled with the bi-directional mechanics to cultivate overlapping nurture. Use your time to share your energy with those in need unconditionally.

Be giving of your time and love, be a facilitator of kindness and courage, and be well!

Joy Begets Joy

The essence of our being is steeped in the kindness and compassion that we all root from in the here and Now. The ability to focus our energies on the connection that is possible with our fellows is where we derive the greatest pleasure.

We learn as we travel through our lives that joy begets joy, and this is achieved when we let go and begin to love. The highest frequency of energetic experiences is opened to us when we shed the low-level vibrations of fear and anxiety.

Our transcendence is made possible when we disconnect from outcomes and the material needs of manifested reality. We are always in possession of what is required to create abundance and happiness by looking deep within and accepting our heart's connection to the grandeur of life.

Be the gratitude that lights your way, be your memoirs as they come to life, and be well!

On Call

We are all here to experience life as it becomes available to us, clarifying the lessons that we have set out to comprehend. Mastery is achieved when our availability status is permanently set to "On Call."

The willingness to allow fluidity to govern our paths will create the least resistance and maximize enjoyment. This state of acceptance will bring with it a natural enthusiasm for every moment as it appears.

The knowledge that our adventure is omnipresent is the spice of life. Transcendence to this high understanding of purposeful universal mechanics creates connections to endless possibilities.

Be exultant in your ability to receive, be confident in your commitment, and be well!

Smile

The window to our souls is said to be through our eyes, and the earthly governor of our demeanor is our ability to control the smiles we share with our fellows. The positioning the corners of our mouths is directly correlated to our sense of well-being and happiness.

Know well that the connection we share is one that stems from our conscious ability to raise our own vibration. The frequency we attune to is the message we communicate with others in a similar space.

Take care to nurture yourself so you can be a light for others. Your words matter and have the opportunity to brighten the path for those in need.

Be the kindness we all require to transcend darkness, be the beacon the world needs to follow the path of light, and be well!

Full Credit for Showing Up

The old saying goes that when the student is ready, the teacher will come. This adage is a universal truth to be held in the highest regard.

The acceptance that teachers come to us in all possible forms is the beginning of opening your heart to an experience that is deeper than the sea and more expansive than the heavens above. The education we receive is formally conveyed to us in the classroom, and then the lessons tested in the school of life as we walk the Earth.

We have the ability to learn from every encounter if we remain receptive to the energy of the course work as is presented to us. The beauty is there is no syllabus and no set rubric for our grading; this class is 100% attendance based.

Allow the universe to be your university and graduation cum laude is assured; you get full credit for showing up. It's truly all about being 100% present in your life to participate and absorb what challenges and victories are bestowed upon you allowing for the expansion of your mind, body and soul.

Be the architect of your personalized curriculum, be first in your class of one, and be well!

The Book of Self

The gospel of the Book of Self is the symphony we create in the essence of our harmonic ability to connect and flourish in the bright light of our soul's expanse. The acceptance of the gifts that have been bestowed upon us are the amplification of our life purpose and its deeper meaning in the universe.

Our path leads us to the lessons we require for our personal growth and its transcended experiences. The manifestation of our mind's eye becomes a portal that aligns our being with our cosmic personification.

Know well that your actions all have grand significance and your loving energy is intended for greatness. Let your knowledge be the light in your life and the calm in your presence.

Be your own biggest fan, be the applause that fills your heart, and be well!

Your Own Knowing

The connection you make to your surroundings is the conduit you maintain to the universe's energy source. The openness that you manifest welcomes in all you need to succeed.

Look no farther than your own knowing to guide your way. The voices you hear are the spirit guides assigned to you to tend to your needs on Earth.

These soul groups have assembled to work toward your highest and best purpose. The shepherding they do is always in alignment with your life's goals.

Listen to what you hear, question what you ponder and act within the light to work to the higher good. Know well that you are protected, guided, and loved.

Be in alignment with what you perceive, be amenable to the extraordinary abundance bestowed upon you, and be well!

Zone of Kindness

The acceptance of our being as we intend ourself to truly be is the path to inner peace and tranquility. When we allow the protective facade to fall away, we find the strength and wherewithal to extend our power beyond the castle walls of our creation.

Know well that we are here to serve others with acts of kindness and gratitude. The gifts we have come from Spirit and this connection is the guiding force that feeds our abilities and nurtures our soul.

As our vibration increases with transcendence, the frequency we attune to elevates in direct correlation. Through the halo we all wear as an antenna, we receive and amplify universal energy.

Please know that as the energetic auric field that is our essence outwardly radiates our persona's intentions, it maintains a physical safe space within our purview for others to receive what we have to graciously offer. This zone of kindness is our present to the kindred spirits on our path.

Allow others to bask in your knowing and presence. This transference of goodwill is the olive branch we all have to offer.

Be the guardian of your inner light, be the purveyor of the joy in your heart, and be well!

Garner Enjoyment

We are the masters of our own domain. The joy that we reserve for ourselves is in direct response to the environment in which we create.

We spend our days in energetic alignment with the perceptions that originate in our mind's eye. The responsibility is ours to be kind to ourselves and all those we enjoy the opportunity to share time and space with in our travels.

The resonant vibration that we emanate is the beacon that calls kindred spirits to our side. Making our life's goal to reside in the higher realm is a gift we grant to ourselves and others.

Know well that you possess the tools to create the happiness you desire. The acceptance of your station in life will garner enjoyment and your response will be enthusiasm.

Owning your own power is the key to manifestation. There are limitlessness possibilities in what the universe has to offer those open to receive.

Be the administrator of your own triumphs, be the catalyst for jubilation, and be well!

Exulted State of Existence

Our sense of self is the grounding point we allow in our earthly form. This inner knowing is the understanding of our innate master plan.

Being in alignment with our higher self is the gateway to the power and glory of the universe. This exulted state of existence is the kindness and compassion that reigns supremely in our hearts when we nurture our connection to the source.

Look no farther than the present moment to grant yourself the assurance that you have all you need to be safe and successful. As your essence melds with that of Spirit, you will receive a heightened sense of awareness.

Know well that as you lessen your self-perpetuated burden, you elevate your frequency and open your coffers to the riches you have in store. The opening you create allows for you to receive the love and light needed to continue on your path of transcendence.

Be the possibilities you see in your mind's eye, be the energy that powers greatness, and be well!

Live in Peace

The world we live in has become dominated by senseless boundaries. The artificial challenges we create can be as easily overcome as they were manifested.

As we embark on our daily journey, we look inward to our priorities to set a course of action. The plan we lay before us is based our knowledge of the skills we possess and the components required to achieve the tasks at hand.

The energy we put forth into our labors is one that is governed by the allocation of our own connection to the source. We are very much aware that the deeper we feel for our project, the more love we expend on its creation.

Time is an earthbound concept that creates disconnection and is aligned with a lower vibration. The understanding that there will always be an abundance of resources to accomplish the vision in your mind's eye is the portal to the high spaces.

The resolve to allow the Now to be all the time you need will gift you the flexibility to live in peace. This construct guarantees durability of action and steadfastness in your productive mindset.

Know well that the sun will rise as well as set on the day's activities. Your presence is all that is required to be successful.

Be in harmony with your surroundings, be in alignment with your moment, and be well!

Duality of Being

Our inner connection to our life plan is the earthbound path that we manifest per our creation. The space we inhabit becomes the playground where we learn and grow.

The knowing that we are always working in our best interest is the ever-present lesson du jour. This understanding is the baseline we must set for the kindness we are responsible to share with ourselves.

Please know in your heart that none of us are infallible and that this internal compassion is the gift we grant unto ourselves. Through this process we allow ourselves the ability to make mistakes and learn from their outcomes.

As we venture onward on our journey, we act as our own teacher and star pupil, all while we hold our heads up high enough to remain in sight of our highest and best purpose. This duality of our being is the exposure we have to our connection to the grander scheme and our symbiotic place within the energetic flow between Heaven and Earth.

Be open to your life's lessons as they present themselves, be compassionate to your cause, and be well!

Life's Secret Sauce

One of the highest compliments that you can pay to someone is to share with them that they obviously care. That's life's secret sauce, the caring within you.

The amount of attention you put into anything has a direct correlation to the quality of its outcome. Tender love and care sets the frequency for any experience.

We all have 100% of our energy to allocate at any moment. We must take great care to align our actions with our goals to achieve the desired results.

Know well that there is no substitute for your full attention. People can sense when you are not engaged and this invariably results in an adjustment in their allocation of focus as a response.

All you truly need to do to be successful is put love into your efforts. The high vibration of loving energy is the catalyst for creativity, connection and completion.

Listen, truly hear people when they speak and look into their eyes when you are with them. This is how words metamorphosize into creation and cooperative actions are spawned.

Be a channel for loving expression in all you do, be positive in your creation, and be well!

Investing in Acceptance

We all have an inner being that we rarely share with the outward world. In fact, there are a large percentage of people who close themselves off to even their own inner understanding.

As we do the work to transcend the issues that we may have traveled here to overcome, or may have created in this incarnation's childhood, we realize that our core persona is the greatest gift we have to offer. The esteem in which we hold our being and its belief systems is the resonance we align to heighten our frequency and connect with our fellows.

As our vibration increases, we attract others in this higher space. The joint tenancy of like-minded conscious souls amplifies the earthy experience and allows for the realization of the portal to the unmanifested realm of Heaven.

Know well that when you invest in the acceptance of your own essence, you elevate all around you. This springboard effect is the calming nurture we all desire to clear our minds and soothe our souls.

Be in acceptance of who you are, be the one to let go and flow with life, and be well!

Alignment to the Light

Aligning ourselves with the higher frequency of goodness allows for a perpetual connection to the source. This understanding brings with it the deeper construct of a universal balance.

The manifested realm is based on a symmetry of light and dark. This equilibrium is achieved by a constant ebb and flow of male and female energies.

Yin and yang are intertwined in a dance that allows for empathy to govern the enlightened spaces. The knowledge that complex forms of life require both the feminine and the masculine for propagation and nurture is an axiom to be held in high regard.

By allowing ourselves the gift to accept that lessons can be learned through non-traditional avenues, we vastly increase the potential foundations for our education. By studying darkness, we can find ways to improve upon the light.

Benefits can be found in all aspects of our lives. The perception we maintain attunes us to the information that is at our disposal.

Welcome the opportunities as they come to you. Retrospect will always provide the growth and healing you require.

Be sympathetic to even the things beyond your scope and understanding, be resolute in your alignment to the light, and be well!

When Friction Dissipates Rhythm Appears

The life we currently live started long before our essence fell to Earth. The knowledge that we chose our path and are here to live its experiences is the acceptance that will soften the lessons yet to come.

As we live, we move through what appears to be a linear progression of time and space. When we let go and allow life to happen, we find the friction dissipates and rhythm appears.

The melody of our soul becomes the soundtrack to our personal master plan. The present moment becomes the screen upon which we view the masterpiece of our own design.

The Now is the parachute that manages the velocity of your experiential descent from moment to moment. The presence you grant yourself will magnify the lessons at hand.

The ability to slow it all down will grant you clarity of mind and action. This zone of control is the space where mastery is achieved.

Be the possibilities you have in your mind's eye, be the master of your own reality, and be well!

Deliberate Energy

So much of what we are able to achieve is based on our attitude. When we align our actions with our goals, we remarkably find that the results we create are perfectly synchronized with the expectations we had in our mind's eye.

The knowledge that we are in complete control of our perspective is all it takes to set the tumblers of the universe in motion. Your active participation in the allocation of your positive energy steers the outcomes you foresee.

If you envision a number line that ranges from -10 to 10, you possess the tools you need to plot your course to success. Establishing a practice to appoint any circumstance a designated positivity ranking on your number line will bring the ordained result to fruition.

When you start every day, you are in the neutral position, the zero on the number line. Those first waking moments allow you to select a personal positivity ranking for the day, and you can rest assured that your wishes will be granted.

Know well that your life is a gift, and you are here to learn what you set out to master. The multifaceted aspects of your experiences are complex by design and all you need to recall is that every moment has significant meaning!

Be deliberate with your energy, be compassionate with your soul, and be well!

Model of Kindness

The master plan we have come here to achieve is one that is a guideline rather than a set of rules and boundaries. We are always open to the free will we have in our mind's eye to experience life as we so choose.

The key to a happy and heathy existence is our ability to steep our essence in love. This highest vibrating of frequencies is the eternal catalyst for compassion and well-being.

Know in your heart that when your life is dedicated to the passion you feel in your soul, you will excel beyond your wildest dreams. The power of the universal source will flow through you and enlighten your way.

Be the composite of all that you know to be good in the world, be the model of kindness for others on their journey, and be well!

Sacred Poses

The image we portray overtly is the outward expression of our resonate vibration. As we interact with our surroundings, we have the opportunity to elevate the landscape through our presence.

The choice we make to maintain residence in the higher realm allows for us to be an energetic lighthouse. The ability to be a beacon for advanced consciousness is an honor for us all to endeavor to achieve.

Physical movement empowers the body and soul. There is a connection between Heaven and Earth that is achieved when endorphins are released through exercise.

Practices like yoga and Tai Chi are fundamentally active meditation. The sacred poses of these disciplines foster energy's movement within our bodies, clearing the path for universal connection and well-being.

Take the time to set your intentional body movements to clearly express your happiness. Sharing your elevated frequency helps raise the ocean for us all.

Be the choreographer of your own personal ballet, be in alignment with universal goodness, and be well!

Life is a Fairy Tale

The passion we have in our hearts to live our lives to their fullest is the translation of our soul's master plan to the manifested realm of earthly expression. This transcendent experience is one that relies on our ability to see past the veneer that shrouds our senses from the magic that is all around us.

The mechanics of the universe are constructed to grant us what we are able to utilize for our highest and best purposes. Please know in your heart that what lays before you is the alchemy of your own design.

Nothing will ever be presented to you without the accompanying ability to create an outcome that aligns with your chosen path. Looking deep within yourself to find the meaning of the lessons as they come to you will grant you the awareness you seek.

The space in which you inhabit is the kingdom in which you reign. Your majesty is solely dependent on the gratitude you anoint to your being.

Life is a fairy tale, and you are its subject and creator. Believing in the enchantment of your own benevolence will unlock the power of the universe for your growth and amazement.

Be the sparkle in your eyes, be aligned with your energetic possibilities, and be well!

Cosmic Tethering

Our engagement on Earth is a limited performance, and we are not simply constricted by rudimentary manifested elements such as time, but by the scope of the awareness we allow ourselves. Our thought processes are deeply aligned with our perceptions of good and evil.

Our actions fall in direct correlation to the algorithms we have built since childhood. The tapes we play in our head are the rewind of that which we have experienced.

The human brain was designed to mirror the universal mindset paradigm of oneness. While the concept of group-think is something that works without flaw in the higher realm, it is not as fluid in the lower spaces.

Daily interaction in the manifested environment requires presence to avoid the energy leak of overthinking. Similar to writing computer code, a leak in energy creates a leak in our ability to maintain a grounding point.

Without this stability, our thought processes wander from one scenario to another, attempting to solve issues with infinite possibilities. Great care must be taken to nurture ourselves to create the ability to draw from the universal source of energy in the present moment to avoid spinning out of control.

The knowledge of what the Now holds is the eternal anchoring point for all of our earthly vessels. Remember to step back and gain perspective granting yourself the gift of a deeper understanding.

Be cosmically in tune with the space in which you are connected, be a tethering post for others in need, and be well!

Assured Presence

The life we create for ourselves is the manifestation of our thoughts as reflected from our inner perceptions of the world around us. This knowledge we have of our environment is of our choice and making.

When we look around, we have the opportunity to see the simplicity of how all the moving parts interrelate, or we can choose to be overwhelmed by the sheer magnitude of it all. The beauty or horror is in the eye of the beholder.

Know in your heart that all that truly matters at any one moment is being presented to you for your immediate consumption. This acceptance of the Now is what grounds you in reality and assures presence of mind and steadfastness of action.

Be aligned with the one truth that meets your higher purpose, be aligned to your soul's well-being, and be well!

Wonder, Amazement and Awe

Wonder, amazement and awe are words we often use to describe the supernatural aspects of our surroundings that are beyond our earthly understanding. This puzzled perspective is one that we realize from an external vantage point.

As we venture onward, we may very well come to an understanding that nothing is exterior to our being. That connection is the highest form of loving energy, and this epiphany is truly worthy of marvel.

The sanctification we create when we bestow the designation of miracle upon an earthly situation is one that opens one's mind to the higher realm of consciousness. When we are willing to align our vibration to this elevated frequency, we close the gap and recognize the oneness that bonds the manifested with the unmanifested dimensions.

Be graceful in your approach to the acceptance of what is, be grateful for the opportunity to serve a higher good, and be well!

Seeing Beyond Ourselves

The essence of our being is the connection we have with our own self-worth. This manifested understanding of our earthly alignment to the master plan is the conduit we maintain to the heavenly realm.

The opportunity to bolster our own inner self-reliance is the strength we garner from the knowledge that we are connected to the universal source. This ability to see beyond introspection is the gift we grant unto ourselves and the world in which we inhabit.

Know well that your purpose on Earth is one that conjoins your being to those kindred spirits in your soul groups as well as the universe's karmic design. This larger picture is the view you see from the upper floors of perception.

Be the loving energy that you require to grow and flourish, be the one who shares your light with others along the way, and be well!

Thematic Perspective

We are here for a purpose, and this reason for being is ours to choose. The commitment we make to this focal point is the ideal by which we live our life.

As we walk the Earth, we emanate a vibration, and its frequency aligns us with others on a similar path. The channel we tune to has a shared resonance that creates a commonality that is held dear by all in the space.

We are attracted to allied travelers through the presence of our chosen signal. As we radiate our thematic perspective, kindred spirits are called to us in reciprocation.

Attuning to kindness, joy and compassion will attract these same elements into your life. Know well that the judgments you make for selecting your demeanor play a huge part in determining those who are in your life.

Be a light worker, be a safe haven for others to take shelter, and be well!

Outwardly Your Inner Best Self

We all stand here today with purpose and a deeper meaning in our life to fulfill. This essence of our eternal being is the grand scope of our master plan.

We arrived here on Earth with a knowing, an inner calling to accomplish. This innate drive is bolstered with gifts that are bestowed upon us to aid us on our quest.

The assurance that we all have from Spirit is that we are never challenged with a circumstance beyond our ability to manifest the best possible outcome. The knowing of our message and course of action is ours to uncover as we travel the path of our making.

Know well that you are a powerful creation and embodiment of the universal source, and this understanding will govern your way. As acceptance fills your soul, a higher frequency is attuned.

The amplification of your vibration manifests a conduit to the ultimate knowledge database of time, space and reality. Your ascension to this hallowed ground of existence becomes the gift you share and the light in your life.

Be outwardly your inner best self, be the strength you require to enhance the world, and be well!

Karmic Kinship

The world we live in is the user interface for the energetic building blocks that constitute the unmanifested universe. The pretense that is universally accepted is that we are all individuals with no binding force to one another.

Upon deeper reckoning, we realize that phenomena like synchronicity are by design. There is a cosmic grid that intertwines us all, and the relationship can be felt on multiple levels of consciousness.

The awareness to transcend the disconnection of isolation leads to a higher space. The epiphany that comes to light is that in the upper realm there is no separation.

When we elevate our understanding to grasp the construct of karmic kinship, we begin to receive the gifts that are intended for us all. The elation that we feel when we share kind words, a gifted smile, or receive the warm embrace of a kindred spirit is the earthy embodiment of heavenly expression.

Know well that you are your brother's brother and sister's sister. There is a euphoria in connection that exists when we welcome others as extensions of our being.

Be aligned to the epic grandeur, be enlightened within, and be well!

Home

We all yearn for safety and security. This inner calling we have to find peace and tranquility is the driving force within our earthly existence.

As we venture onward in our lives, we never lose site of the path we have taken to reach the space we now inhabit. The steps walked have forged the shelter we call home.

Please know that home is not necessarily a physical place. It is the amalgamation of our positive experiences that fills our heart and grants us peace of mind while shining light on the unknown that lays before us.

As we create our life by placing one foot in front of the other, we journey toward the light we see in our mind's eye. This adventure takes us homeward bound regardless of the course we plot or the destination achieved.

The simple knowing that wherever you land you will have the comfort to be at ease in your own being is the sanctified space we joyfully call home. Your essence will always provide you the tools, strength and opportunity to glean the very best for yourself in alignment with your master plan.

Be compassionate with your outreach, be the traveler with purpose and an outstretched hand, and be well!

Aligning Goals and Actions

Purpose and perspective are the key elements in grounding. These two components work systematically to clear the manifested path for energy to flow from on high.

As we align our goals with our actions, we find that our methods yield fruit. The paydirt we hit is based on our ability to raise our consciousness to the heights that transcend fear.

The vantage point we gain from the penthouse view is one that allows for connection to all that the universe has to offer. The grand scope of your life's intentions are always within your reach.

Know well that your capacity for love and happiness is truly yours for the creation. Letting go of what ails you is as simple as accepting it for what it is and releasing it to the ether.

Be the one to chart your course above the fog of fear, be the pilot of your flight to the destinations of your calling, and be well!

Blueprints for Actions

One of the most honored roles we play in life is the opportunity to teach and mentor others on their paths. This hallowed space is one to be treated with the utmost reverence.

We all play the sometimes interchangeable parts of student and teacher throughout our lives, and as we share our experiences we must take every effort to impart wisdom with the kindness we wish it to be received. Openness of mind is a bidirectional conduit that must be shared by both parties if a true symbiosis is to be realized.

Knowledge is the key to success and happiness. Through our connection to our fellow travelers, we achieve the elevation to the higher consciousness that exists when we fulfill the need to serve.

Know well that your intentions are the blueprints for your actions and they work hand in hand to manifest your desired results. Our essence is the gift we pay forward with our kind gestures of heart and soul.

Be a purveyor of goodwill and light, be the empowerment for the transference of energetic knowledge, and be well!

Bi-Directional Energy

Awareness is a gift we grant ourselves. The grace our path takes is a cognizant decision we make moment to moment.

As we journey, we learn from our experiences. The interactions we have and the connections we establish are based on the level of consciousness to which we are attuned.

The fellow travelers we share time with on Earth are all kindred spirts in vibration. These angels bestow upon us the light we need to find our way.

Please know that every other being and the lessons they share have meaning that is crucial to our growth. Energy is bi-directional, and the law of attraction assures us that our thoughtful intentions are guaranteed to be rewarded through kindness.

Be present, be conscious in your perception, and be well!

Highlight the Good

The ability to highlight the good in our lives is the cherished gift we grant unto ourselves. The opportunity is always here for us to be grateful for our many blessings and light our way with their grandeur.

Know in your heart that the lessons we learn and the people we meet are the paving stones for the path we walk. This creation of our design is the road to our inner happiness.

When we shine from the inside, we become a beacon of loving kindness that draws others to our side and fulfills our needs for companionship. Through this connection we elevate our vibration and expand the collective consciousness.

The attunement to the frequency of energetic love becomes the promised land of Heaven on Earth. Know well that the choice is always yours to decide which fork in the road leads to the state of mind that feeds your soul.

Be the brightness that brings a smile to your face, be the kindness that others welcome into their lives, and be well!

Ready to Receive

The vantage point that we hold in life is aligned with the frequency to which we are attuned. Here on Earth, the knowledge that is readily available to us will vary greatly depending on the intentions we set.

As we seek, we journey through the lens of our design. The clarity that we gain is in direct correlation with the vibration we emanate.

The halls we walk are filled with travelers in a similar space. The interaction we beckon towards us fulfills our need to stabilize our current thought processes.

As our consciousness permits alignment with external visions, a symbiosis occurs. The alchemy we undertake opens our mind to the epiphany of new ideas and understandings that may have eluded us in the past.

The open door we walk through is a portal. The access we gain is a promotion to a higher space of connection and well-being.

Be poised to look beyond what you thought you knew, be the conduit to welcome the greater good, and be well!

Unnecessary Formalities

Deep within our very being is the essence of our soul's knowing. This inner space is the embodiment of our purposeful existence.

As we mature in our earthly incarnation, we are granted the attunements we desire. These amplified experiences become the frequency to which we align.

The gift we bestow upon ourselves is the ability to communicate our needs and desires to the others in our circle. This connection comes in all forms as we transcend.

As we reach the highest levels of consciousness, we come to the understanding that verbal communication is an unnecessary formality. Our vibration shares our thoughts as if the words were shouted from the mountaintops.

Know in your heart that your wishes will be heard loud and clear in the higher realm. Your resonation of love will speak its volumes to all.

Be sanctified in your actions, be clear with your intentions, and be well!

A World Beyond Ourselves

Our belief systems are comprised of the learned behaviors we have absorbed during our earthly trajectory. Starting with our earliest sensory inputs on through our formative years, we have learned what to believe from our parents, friends, teachers, and the general ecosystem.

As toddlers, we start to realize that there is a world beyond ourselves, and as maturity blossoms, a feeling of belonging becomes paramount for the development of our self-worth. When the notion that there is something bigger than us becomes the overarching theme, an overwhelmed or tranquil mindset may become prevalent depending on perspective.

Connection to the source energy plays an enormous role in how we perceive ourselves, others, and the world around us. When we are tied into the cosmic grid, we derive a knowing that the universe is here to provide for us if we are open to receive.

Faith in the philosophy of your choosing is a stabilizing factor. Please know well that any dogmatic approach to anything will isolate you and this should never be the goal.

Embracing your own views is empowering. The acceptance of other's ideals is enlightening.

Be part of the whole, be accepting of the variables that comprise the equation, and be well!

Gifted Moments

We wake in the morning looking for the meaning we must assign to the day's events that lay before us. This understanding we search for is the essence of our lives and the light we look to have illuminate our way.

There are experiences we encounter that resonate more deeply than others. These moments are no more sacred than all the others, but they strike an individual chord that vibrates deeply within our soul.

This connection we make to our life plan aligns our earthly existence with our heavenly purpose. Through this process we elevate our consciousness to accept that our waking moments are all gifted to us so that we may grow metaphysically and nurture others under Spirit's loving guidance.

Be the empowerment to others you feel in your very core, be the confluence of mind, body and soul that the world needs to transcend, and be well!

Mapping the Voyage

As we return to our bodies from our night's adventure in the unmanifested realm of dreams and unbridled connection, we have the opportunity to bring that bliss back to Earth. As your eyes open, remember that your initial thoughts and intentions set your course for the day's events.

Mapping the voyage for your exploration of experiences is yours for the creation. Welcome your first glimpses of daylight with a smile and a laugh, and the world is guaranteed to giggle along with you in support of your happiness.

Finding the enjoyment in everything you do elevates your vibration and attunes you to others on that same frequency. Set your intention to resonate in the higher space and feel the energy within you flow naturally.

Be the genesis of your rapture, be the purveyor of goodwill, and be well!

The Role We Play

Every instance of our lives has meaning and purpose. The interactions we have and the lessons we learn are all part of a grander plan that has been running in the background of our life from birth.

This understanding allows for us to be at ease in our daily existence without the concern that we may misstep or miss out on an opportunity that is meant for us to undergo as part of the master plan. Know in your heart that you are at the exact right place at the perfect time to fulfill your karmic aspirations.

The role we play in the grandeur of the universe is more epic than we may fully give ourselves credit for as cast members. Grant yourself the mindful awareness that your presence is an integral part of the equation as a constant rather than a variable.

Know in your soul that it's all going according to plan and the mapping of your life is as fluid as you wish it to be. The designs you sketch are never in stone and all are anchored in your fundamental well-being.

Be the surveyor of your own space, be in-line with your personal reality, and be well!

Universal Fluidity

The cells in our bodies are vigilantly awaiting the stimuli that signals their appropriate response. This process on the manifested micro-level is a complex set of chemical chain reactions triggered by our perception.

What we perceive is the fulcrum in our ability to ground ourselves. When we are connected to the unmanifested space, we are in alignment with universal fluidity.

Please know that a healthy cell is one that is fluid and pliable in its ability to act. Rigidity occurs at the molecular level when elasticity is lost due to a low-level vibration that aligns to negativity and fear.

The key to a long and happy life is to create a baseline for your reality that is steeped in the light. When your go-to viewpoint is anchored in goodness, your thought patterns will follow suit.

Take in every conscious breath knowing that you are in a safe and relaxed space where the present moment holds all you need for success. Life is a game for you to play, and enjoy what you have the opportunity to learn and share.

Be yourself, be proud of who you are, and be well!

Imprinting Love

As we have matured, we have graduated from one set of circumstances to the next, learning valuable lessons along the way. This process of maturation has drawn its power from your symbiotic connection to the universal source of loving energy.

When we start out in our earthly existence, we inherently bond with our caregivers. This energetic exchange is our first taste of what we refer to as love in the manifested realm of reality.

The love we feel is what we embody as safety, security and joy. As we matriculate through life's ever-changing roles and responsibilities, the needs and meaning of the space love plays in our world changes along with it.

Please know in your heart that love is an environmental constant and your ability to find it is readily available at all times. The baseline you created in your earliest days is the imprinting you can always refer to where you will always be safe and enjoy peace of mind.

Rest assured that your lessons learned have granted you the self-assurance that has become yours forevermore. This grounding is what allows you to share your true essence with others who practice these gifted teachings on the same frequency.

Be a student of this school of loving kindness, be the compassion that lights the world, and be well!

Those You Love

As we walk the Earth, we create a network of like-minded souls, learning and growing in correlation to our experiences. These fellow travelers all resonate in their own vibration with overlaps in frequency attuned to our own.

As we move throughout our days, we continue to attract others to our cause based on our emanation. This beacon lights the way for goodness to amass.

There is no need to look to the sky to locate your angels. They are right here with you!

The team we have the honor to build are our guiding lights. Our family, friends and the kindred souls we share time and space with in our lives are Heaven-sent to help us complete our journey.

Open your mind to the concept of Heaven here on Earth. As you raise your elevation, more and more of the divine opens and becomes accessible.

Rest assured your angels will find you. There is only connection to their loving kindness and assistance in the higher realm.

Be surrounded by those you love, be proactive in what goodness you manifest, and be well!

Trueness of Possibility

What we think we know may actually be limiting what we have the ability to perceive. The knowledge that we have amassed while here on Earth is governed by the constructs of our design.

Know well that there is always more than meets the eye. Our ability to receive a deeper understanding is dependent on the connection we maintain with the source.

The limitations we place on our perceptions is an unnecessary constriction that relies on our mind's insistent need to label all we see. When we tag and categorize all we encounter, we limit our ability to experience the true essence of what lays before us.

The words we assign to our visional interactions correlate to a surface level understanding, and thereby inhibit the free flow of energy that embodies the trueness of possibility. When we allow mana to inhabit the auric field as it intends, we receive the full presence of people, animals, objects, places and even situations.

Be assured that what you see is always a portal to more, be open to the expanse, and be well!

Elevated Vantage Point

Our sense of self may be our most prized possession. The ability to position one's mindset to create an internally nurturing bionetwork is paramount to health and happiness.

As we go about our business, we encounter a myriad of opportunities to judge ourselves and others. When these occasions arise, grant yourself the perspective to step back and see the bigger picture from an elevated vantage point.

From on high, you will see that none of it is that serious. That bird's eye view will make it abundantly clear that you have a choice in how you react and ultimately feel.

When we attune our understanding to a higher vibration, we are able to find the humor in almost anything. The ability to see how silly a situation is or even how humorous our reactions were allows us the ultimate gift of laughter.

There is nothing more healing than a smile or a good laugh. When the basis of our amusement comes from the most personal of sources, it acts as the best medicine.

Be the creation of your own delight, be aligned with your own potential for joy, and be well!

Unlocking Consciousness

We enter our lives with the full capacity for our very being. This original baseline is manifested from our full essence and energetic blueprint.

As we experience the lessons we call to ourselves, we open our awareness to the deeper levels of our own existence. This transformation is the process we call life.

Know well that as we chronologically mature, we simply unlock the multifaceted levels of our consciousness that have been present since inception. Our karmic DNA is preordained, and we are the blessed recipient of what is in store.

Be the blossoming life force that is intended for your higher and best purpose, be the positive energy that feeds your soul, and be well!

Realism's Sliding Baseline

Reality is a state of mind, and the province in which you take up residence is of your choosing. The awareness you perceive becomes your grounding point for introspection.

As beings of presence, we generate a sense of mindfulness in correlation with the alignment we have to our momentary surroundings. The essence of our well-being is intertwined with connection to the higher source.

The foundation of our truth is our work of genius to create. That being held in high regard, the life we choose is ours based on the intentions we manifest.

Realism has a sliding baseline, and its anchor point is as personal as a fingerprint. The pressures of our lives are generally of our own conception.

Be aloof to the drama, be your own sense of actuality, and be well!

More Than the Space We Inhabit

At a hopeful young age, we are taught the fine art of the hug. This tool of earthly connection is the gift that embraces our core energies at the root of their being.

Our purposeful interaction is multifaceted to say the very least. It is a complex vibrational exchange with its intentions deeply intertwined in the essence of those involved.

When we touch another human being, we exchange energy, and this neurological firing of synapses gives birth to the related emotional response. The range of reaction is based on the openness of the participants ability and willingness to receive the vibrations manifested.

Know well that when we interlock our auric field with another being, we share more than the space we inhabit. We momentarily align frequency and through this connection relationship is born.

Be openly giving of your soul's intent, be willing to receive love as it is shared, and be well!

Suffering is Optional

Life need not be as serious as most people make it. We are here to learn and grow; the suffering is optional.

Our vibration is the attraction we have to other travelers, and the situations we manifest are the result of our elections. The frequency we attune to is as simple as turning the dial to the channel of your choosing.

We must take great care to place ourselves at a karmic elevation that works to our higher purpose. It's as simple as pressing the floor selection button in an elevator.

Every morning when you wake, make the conscious decision to press the "PH" button for your trip up to the Penthouse. The view is amazing and laughter fills the air.

Know well that the wealth of your existence merely depends on the kindness you show yourself. Grant yourself the gift of laughter; it's the fastest way to raise your vibration!

Be good to yourself, be in a state of amusement, and be well!

Inventory of Perception

The essence of our being is the lifeline we create between ourselves and the grander purpose we have come to Earth to achieve. The master plan of our soul is the true north that is the constant in the life we are blessed to create.

Know in your heart that what we perceive in our daily existence will be used as the baseline against which we measure all aspects of our interactions. This understanding grants us the power to preside over our lives with the care and compassion we deserve.

The kindness we share with ourselves is the mirror we reflect upon others. Take the time to do your own inventory of perception so its inner beauty may shine on your outward existence.

Be the creator of your own reality, be the light that brightens other's experiences, and be well!

Welcoming Presence

The manifested world we live in is in a constant state of movement. The energy that flows to us is a bi-directional homing beacon that connects Heaven and Earth.

Our busy lifestyles may disconnect us from the opportunity to remain grounded. It is our responsibility to maintain connection.

Within stillness we find the answers. Allow yourself the time and personal space for quiet meditation and reflection.

If there are any questions in your life, you can rely on your own personal deeper understanding to show you the way. Your ability to draw from the source is an innate power.

Quiet your mind, relax your body and listen to the universe. A smile on your face and an openness of your heart is all you need to welcome in presence and attune to the frequency of your choosing to fulfill your quest.

Be aligned with the vastness that is mindfulness, be attuned to the higher frequency of your calling, and be well!

Fundamental Choices

We all have fundamental choices to make in our moment-to-moment experience. The decisions we are faced with are comprised of the sensory inputs we digest and how we choose to allow what we glean to determine our actions and reactions.

The baseline we build becomes our grounding, or a protective buffer. The opportunity is always ours to set our own parameters for the messaging we take in as fact versus fiction.

When we make the decision to open our soul to the frequency of truth, we align our essence to the waking state of enlightenment. This powerful gift we grant ourselves is one that elevates our consciousness and allows for us to become who we have always intended to be.

Know well that you need only live in the light of your own kindness and compassion. This space will manifest the trueness you require to flourish and be happy.

Be empowered in your awakened state, be the consciousness of your creation, and be well!

Productive Circles

Our perspective on life is directly correlated to the frequency to which we are attuned. This vibratory experience is the governance that the universe places on the manifested realm to ensure that soul groups are enabled to travel in productive circles.

The reality of the quantum mechanics is that we align our outcomes with the intentions we set. The work rests within our purview to create the alignment between our actions and our goals.

The desire to do great things is only the foundation of the process. We must have the courage to let go of what we believe we know to make room for the vulnerability to accept what we do not know.

As we transcend fear and embrace the present moment, we allow for the formation of ourselves incarnate. Bravery is directly drawn from the source and allows for a free flow of information and its exchange with those in need.

A creative side exists within us all, and this artisan resides deeply in our core. Compassion and creativity are at the roots of all that is good, as it illuminates the way for those open to the challenge.

Be brave, be within yourself as you connect to the unmanifested space, and be well!

Maintaining Connection

There is a calling we all have from deep within ourselves to maintain connection to the source of all life. This understanding we innately have is our ability to see beyond ourselves and bond with the oneness that binds the fibers of the universe.

Looking in the mirror allows us to see the reflection of our earthly incarnation as well as the portal to the vastness of the unmanifested realm. Our eyes are the gateway to our soul, and this pathway leads to that of all creation.

Know in your heart that your essence is that of something much greater than you alone. We are all akin to one another, and our energy is a shared resource at its core.

The time we spend learning to love our fellows is that which elevates us all. Your acceptance of a symbiotic reality is the cornerstone of transcendence.

Be aligned with what is bigger than us all, be the sum of the parts, and be well!

The Zone

Our lives operate in a synchronistic state of existence with the universe. The concert we call life is the opus of our creation and is truly a masterpiece.

When we slow down long enough to feel the earth beneath our feet, we realize that our grounding points surround us. The trees, clouds and air envelop us with nurturing energy allowing us to create and foster bonds with our cohorts.

As we learn to let go and allow connection to the source govern our earthly movements, a sense of harmony raises our vibration and our frequency attunes to a higher channel. The naturally flowing feeling of being in the zone is where everything is possible.

Slow your mind, open your soul, and sway with the inaudible cosmic soundtrack. The dance is in perfect alignment with your personal symphony.

Be the rhythm in your life, feel the connection, and be well!

Energetic Programming

Our thoughts are the energetic programming we use to align our earthly perceptions with our connection to the universal source. This bi-directional exchange is the grounding we depend upon to bring forth the power available to us all.

The highest vibration is that of love and gratitude. When we allow ourselves to resonate in this space, we open our experiences to the kindness and compassion that reigns in the higher realm.

Look upon yourself as a purveyor of goodwill, and you will gladly share its guidance and be protected by its light. Know in your heart that as you look upward to the sky in prayer that your vibration emanates toward the heavens as well as to your cohort on Earth.

Be a conduit for the goodness you feel in your soul, be the beacon to aid others on their way, and be well!

Boundless Opportunities

The alignment we create with our personal peace is not one that is based on the spoils reaped from our encounters here on Earth. The internal joy we manifest comes from how deeply we learn to connect with others.

The experiences we all have are intertwined. The interrelated web that the universe weaves brings the willing participants into the foreground, best served for the traveler open to receive.

The intentions we set are the guidelines the cosmos relies on to map our course. Mindful interaction with your daily life practices opens you to boundless opportunities.

The knowledge that good extends beyond our own auric field is the first step in welcoming in goodness and prosperity. An extended hand and offer to help others in need is the greatest blessing we can bestow on ourselves and those we have the honor to know and love.

Be aligned with those around you, be in awe of the magic you create, and be well!

Managing Overthinking

The life we live is one that is filled with the experiential learning that is designed to fill our soul with knowledge and overcome the challenges that we have faced previously. As we venture onward, we may always trust in our ability to draw on Spirit's energy to guide our way even when we faulter.

As humans, we are all faced with the task of managing the overthinking that plagues our perception. Remaining present allows for our connection to the source to ground and keep us in the light.

Know in your heart that you have what it takes to do the needful. Trust in your soul to illuminate the way and overcome any negativity you may encounter.

Be brave, be in the Now, and be well!

Daily Calculations

Our outlook on life is the most critical element of our personal well-being. The perspective we create through our alignment with our surroundings chooses the frequency of our vibrations.

The choices we make, the kindred spirits in our circle and the plans we create set the roadmap for our journey. These variables all make up the equation that we work hard to calculate daily.

The beauty of our existence is that our perceptions are all set by our free will. This open-source code is as personal or as collaborative as you wish it to be.

Look no farther than what is before your eyes or in your soul to determine what baseline suits your higher purpose. The knowing is within you and this knowledge comes to you as freely as does your own consciousness.

The happiness in the world is yours to create, the perpetuating voyage remains yours to sail and the grand outcome always yours to manifest.

Be cognizant, be proactive, and be well!

Seek the Best for Yourself

We are the mirror of our own thoughts, and the life we manifest is 100% dependent on those perceptions. Know in your heart that you control your reality, and its projection is always of your design.

The key to happiness and physical well-being lies deep within you. Self-realization is all that is required to allow yourself the gift of inner compassion and serenity.

Seek the best for yourself, and when you do, you will align with others in a similar space. This symbiosis is the magic that unites like-minded souls and raises the collective vibration for us all.

Be kind to yourself so you can radiate love outwardly, be the master of your own time, space and reality, and be well!

Catalyst for Connection

Communication is one of the strongest catalysts for connection. The means by which we share our thoughts and intentions is the grandest of energetic exchanges.

Our aura radiates the vibration of our intent. The spiritual observer is aware of the emanation presented in their presence.

As we interact with our fellow travelers, we must be mindful of the goal of our assembly. As we amass manifested energy in a geographic location, a powerful pooled frequency booster is created, and this beacon opens a portal.

This unlocked doorway leads to the reality aligned to the vibration of the frequency attuned to the group-think. Positive energy will always overshadow darkness, but please know that if negativity is chosen as the baseline in the earthly realm, it too will generate negativity in propagation.

Know well that what we share with others via word, thought and action is an extension of our higher self, and our belief systems are directly allied with the unmanifested space. Being conscious of the source from which you draw you power is paramount to your success.

Be honest in your intent, be true in your existence, and be well!

Wholehearted Acceptance

The life we live has purpose that draws its energy from the grandest of sources. The wholehearted acceptance that your faith can be placed firmly in your inner knowing is the gift you may grant yourself.

The path we walk is not preordained, and its rudder is yours to maintain. Allowing the universe to run its course without your undue resistance opens your experience to the expanse that lies before you.

We have a responsibility to work toward our highest and best purpose. This charter is one that sees us focus on the full scope of our experience rather than any narrow task.

Know in your heart that our energy is best utilized when it is allowed to follow a path that is natural and without resistance. Go with the flow, and the current will lead to the desired destination.

Be the master of your voyage, be the strength that allows you to let go, and be well!

The Linear Illusion of Time

The manifested environment has its anchor points in the low vibrations that create the physical realm. The tangible perspective that generates this facade is one that allows for an earthly sense of grounding and perspective.

Within our domain resides the core tenets from which we construct our sense of reality. This life we build for ourselves is our shelter, and hopefully gives us the solace to live in peace.

Our path is in constant flux. The ebb and flow are the catalysts for interaction and movement.

The progression of the linear illusion of time manifests altered states of presence, and these modifications warrant our attention. The responsibility falls on us to allow ourselves the flexibility to modulate our frequency, allowing for change in physical attachment.

The variance in our abilities to distinguish between loss and gain is directly correlated to the baseline of our sense of self-worth. Knowing well that your deeper connection is the source of your innate value allows for an attuning to a higher vibration and your resonate frequency to transcend fear.

Be fluid in your thoughts, be open to what life brings you, and be well!

Sanctify Your Existence

Happiness is the most sought after of all commodities on Earth. This elusive state of mind is always here for you to choose.

Look no farther than your own perception to ground and sanctify your existence. We are here to learn, and the most important lesson is to be kind to yourself.

When you allow yourself the compassion to forgive and move past any issues you may have encountered, you allow your life lessons to resonate. There is never a circumstance that arises that does not have a silver lining.

It is our mission in life to find the bright side and share that wealth with others. Know well that a smile and a kind word are the blessing you can bestow on anyone you are granted to honor to meet along the way.

Be the joy others seek to feel safe and complete, be the light that shines for you and the ones you love, and be well!

Gaining Perspective

We come into this world with a clean slate and an understanding that everything we see in front of us is part of a larger picture in alignment within the deep connection between the manifested and unmanifested environments. As we mature, our interactions with our fellow travelers creates a readjustment of our frequency based upon the perceptions we create.

The testing ground that we call Earth is merely a sandbox for our own growth experiences geared toward universal betterment. As we transcend the challenges that we came here to work through, we gain perspective toward enlightenment.

Our ultimate purpose on this planet is to spread kindness and joy. The ability to share what we have learned is the ultimate gift.

When we come in contact with someone who is less fortunate than ourselves, it is our karmic duty to bequeath upon them what light has shined upon us. The tools we have at our disposal are as plentiful as we choose.

Your kind gestures are always impactful. Your well-intended smile has the ability to transform another's view of themselves and the world in which they live.

Be a messenger for the higher frequency, be a conduit for goodness, and be well!

Cohort of Companionship

The beauty in the world comes from the love and compassion we share with our fellows. The connection we create is the energy that welcomes Heaven's light to our earthly existence.

As we build our cohort of companionship, we elevate our frequency and align it with the universal source. This amalgamation of life force and understanding is the mortar between the bricks that fortify our soul.

The joy we manifest in our daily lives is created from our perceptions and interactions. The essence of our reality is the kindness we allot ourselves through the desire to elevate the collective.

The space in which you reside is the domain you have created to bolster Spirit's illumination. Know well that the ability to bring a smile to other's faces resides within you and your tender embrace of those you love.

Be open to share what you have learned along the way, be the positive signpost others may seek, and be well!

Happiness is a State of Mind

Happiness is a state of mind. The perceptions we manifest are the reality of our choosing.

A smile or laughter can change the course of any situation's trajectory. Our willingness to find, or even create the bright side, is the key to success.

Know well that the facade that we see in any circumstance is 100% pliable to our will and the energy we emit in its resonant space. We are the masters of our own reality in all levels of consciousness.

Be attuned to your own knowing, be aligned with the goodness around you, and be well!

Unexplored Parts of Yourself

We are raised from our early childhood with a sense of self. This knowledge of who we are meant to be is merely the outward persona we defer to on Earth.

As we learn and mature, we realize the connection we have to the grander scheme of the universe and the larger role we play on the stage of life's existence. This attachment we share with our fellow travelers is what enhances our lives and brings us love and happiness.

Look to those who you know and trust for a caring and helping hand. See the opportunity in every circumstance to grow and expand your being.

The others you look on as strangers are truly just unexplored parts of yourself. Open your heart and your wholeness will blossom.

Be one with the essence of Spirit that surrounds us, be mindful of your connection, and be well!

Traveler's Blessing

The connection we feel with the other earthbound travelers is a blessing. The opportunity to share time, space and energy is a gift that is forever replenished by Spirit to nurture our soul.

Interaction is the construct that enables higher consciousness, and this ability to collaborate bonds us all at the deepest of levels. The manifested realm is one that relies heavily on physical contact to align our frequencies through rudimentary connective expressions of relation, like handshakes or hugs.

This overt exchange of unmanifested energy creates momentary alignment and ushers in a sense of warmth and a symbiosis in being. Know well that your gestures of kindness will be well received, as the vibration of an outstretched hand or an embrace is universally revered as a sign of peace and prosperity.

Be sincere, be the facilitator of compassion, and be well!

Our Open-Ended Experience

Our life is an open-ended experience that has no limitations or requirements. The guidance we seek comes to us in the form of the path we choose.

The ability to raise our consciousness above perceptual boundaries is the gift we grant ourselves. The knowledge we glean is allotted to us as we formulate the curriculum of our earthly incarnation.

Open your mind to the vastness of the possibilities that surround you. The universe is an intentional playground of sights, sounds and adventures for you to bask in as you evolve and flourish.

Be the best you you can imagine, be the self you have always known to be true, and be well!

Replenish Your Soul

The world we live in is intentionally a challenge. The hurdles we face are lessons that are custom made for our growth.

The school of life is based on a curriculum that requires balance to achieve success. Everything we experience is designed to create connection.

This construction is mapped to both Heaven and Earth. The concrete jungle most of us reside within inhibits energy flow and thereby constricts our ability to draw from the source.

Thought and the human condition are earthly manifestations that divert energy away from the present moment. The Now is the only true conduit to reality and peace.

As our lives fall deeper into the manifested realm, great intentional lengths must be taken to foster the bi-directional connection to the unmanifested space. The simplest way to plug into the zero-point field is through nature.

Letting go of thinking through mediation will open your soul. Focusing on your breath as your only concentration will release your earthbound ties.

A forest is a nice to have but all you need is a park, a tree or even a patch of grass to connect and ground yourself to more than meets the eye to replenish your soul.

Be part of the flow, be in tune with the source, and be well!

No Perfunctory Moments

The path we walk is by design the life we are meant to live. The lessons we learn and the souls we interact with are the curriculum of our master plan.

The knowledge we glean along the way is the gift we have come here to receive. The metamorphosis we undertake is the journey toward our highest and best self.

There is no perfunctory moment in time. Every encounter we experience is interrelated to our grander purpose.

Have faith in your choices, as they all are stepping stones to the next. Your way is the adventure of your choosing and its manifestation is your essence.

Be in alignment with your known calling, be open to the frequency to which you attune, and be well!

Quantum Events

Our lives are a string of quantum events that are the amalgamation of the connected perceptions we have manifested. The observations we have drawn as we walk our path are the trigger points that ignite the engines of creativity and ingenuity.

The connection we have with our fellow travelers fans tiny flames into the bonfires that warm our hearts and forge bonds with kindred spirits. The thoughts we share are the unmanifested dendrites that are the conductors of a larger consciousness.

As energy travels it carries with it a vibration. The frequency to which it is attuned acts as a guidance system for the path of energetic travel that determines the termination point of the message in flight.

Some may hear the message, some deeply feel its intent and others may only know words were shared. Know well that while the story may be told, only those in alignment are blessed with its meaning.

Allow the emotion around you to enlighten you with its purpose. Your innate ability to align with your desired attunement will protect and guide you.

Be aligned with those in your space, be a pleasant conduit for the transference of knowledge, and be well!

Manifest the Calling in Your Heart

Our life purpose is to learn, grow and love based on the freedom we grant unto ourselves to be who we really know ourselves to be. When we allow our true essence to reign over our lives, the majesty of our being comes into the light for all to see.

The energy we have within us is gifted to manifest the calling in our hearts. The choice is always ours to allot this heavenly power as we see fit.

The knowing that the universal source is ours to wield as a tool grants us the power to create the vision we have in our mind's eye. This sacred space is the protection we build as we nurture our soul.

Know well that your thought controls your being and the foreseen outcomes will follow suit. Spend your mind's power in the light so that your path will be one of joyful experiences.

The process is yours to manage. Keep your head up high and visions even higher.

Be without worry and concern, be happy with your self-realization, and be well!

Time and Maturity

The way we live our lives is a choice. We always have options, and the alternatives we are offered range based on the vastness of our ability to perceive.

The time we spend on Earth allows for a harvesting of knowledge and a sharpening of our senses. The skills we garner create the breadth of opportunity we rely on to build the success criteria for our well-being.

As the scope of our understanding forms its framework, we are gifted with the ability to separate the wheat from the chaff. Time and maturity lend us the capacity to see what is in our best interest and what needs to be discarded.

The tools are here for our use. It's as simple as making the conscious decision to live in the light versus darkness.

This beacon calls to you the energy of your choosing, and the universe will present itself in that likeness without fail. Know well that being positive will generate a boomerang effect, and your creation will respond in kind.

Be a light, be an optimist, and be well!

Loaded for Bear

Some live life as if they were here to survive the experience while others realize that we are here to capture the essence of the journey in our hearts and infuse it with the power in our souls. Herein lies the key to living life to its fullest, rather than simply existing.

The being that we create is the target we set. The aim we envision is the purview of our imagination.

Seeing beyond the landscape before us expands our scope and opens our possibilities to the grandeur of the universe. Know in your heart that nothing is off the table, and that you are fully loaded for bear!

Be the one who reaches past the designed mile markers, be what you cherish most in life, and be well!

The Self-Governing Contract

We come into this world with a plan, a mission that was conceived with a deeper purpose that we may recall. Our behavior from a young age is indicative of the contract we have with ourselves.

The innate course of action we feel compelled to observe is hardwired. We may refer to it as personality traits or genetics, when in reality it was a conscious decision we made to be who we are in alignment with the goals we seek.

The community we create is a manifestation of the vibration we align to, and this tribe is one that resonates in concurrence. This shared frequency fosters an accord of commonality in purpose and disposition.

Having the courage to be you is the bravest of all achievements. The overt knowledge that you have gleaned is the commitment to your life purpose and can be claimed as success at the most primal of levels.

Be aware of what grounds you, be the facilitator of your space, and be well!

Our Biological Essence

The cells that make up the physical body are connected through the DNA that is their biological essence, as well as the sensory input they receive in their moment-to-moment experience by our perceptions. This ever-present flow of data forms the reality of our choosing.

The internal condition we manifest is based on our outward perspective. Our chemistry is dependent upon our moods, and these emotions guide the earthly biology within us.

Know in your heart that your own well-being is dependent on the environment of your making. Your physical health is intertwined with your understanding and acceptance of your surroundings.

Be the safe harbor for your mind's assurance, be the space in which you may rest, and be well!

Our Construction

We are the masters of our own domain. From the time we wake in the morning to the moment we drift off to our dream state of higher consciousness, we are in complete control.

The acceptance that our perceptions govern our emotions is the gateway to holding the reins of our own actions and well-being. We have the ability to align our vibration to the frequency of our choosing through an overt process.

Our decision-making procedure is one of our construction. We utilize the success criterion that we have amassed through our manifested life experiences while incorporating the unmanifested source code we have drawn for our consumption.

We align our goals to our master plan and develop our happiness quotient based on the needed endorphins required to sustain our comfort and security. These core beliefs and their associated social responsibilities are the seeds we sow that allow for the universal connection with the energy that is life and all that is divine.

Be in bliss, be the creator of your own sanctified space, and be well!

Treading Lightly

The connection we have to our environment is one that emanates deeply from our soul's manifestation. This outreach is one that stems from word, action and intent.

Know in your heart that the vibration you radiate is the overt aura that you share with the world in which you live. This sacred space is the shelter we create for ourselves and those we welcome into our covenant no matter the duration.

As we walk the Earth, we have a responsibility to tread lightly and enhance the experience for others in our wake. The gift we are blessed to share with our fellow travelers is one of kindness and compassion.

Be aware of your power, be a creator of goodness wherever you may be, and be well!

You at Play

When was the last time you simply did something for its pure sense of enjoyment? Ask yourself – do you have the short-term capacity to let go of all the responsibilities that adulthood has bestowed upon you?

For most, when we were children, we woke without serious burden and carried out our day's agenda under the blissful protection of presence. This carefree environment fostered a joyful existence that nurtured our souls while creating connection to the universe.

This free-form ability to be in a sanctified space opened our psyche to the prevailing energies that empowered us to skip, dance and sing to our heart's content. The higher vibration that resonates in youth lends to creativity and expansion on one's ability to perceive at a higher cognitive level.

As we mature, we amass the obligations of the persona we create. In general, the common school of thought is that "I'm too busy," or "I'm too important," or "I'm too dignified" to allow your inner child any daylight. This path is one that leads away from who you truly are as a person.

The you of your earlier days was the real you and this creation of latter years is the facade you manifested to suit an external need to impress someone other than yourself. Allowing yourself to be yourself will unleash the core of your personality and unlock the creative side that had been suppressed at your own hand.

It's time to reclaim your essence. It's time to be truly at home in your presence and be one with your artistic being.

Be you at play, be open to what happens next, and be well!

Methodical Chaos

The universe in which we live has an order to it, and this set of rules can best be described by the esoteric concept of methodical chaos. There is no defined right or wrong, but there is an underlying mechanical basis for its process.

The knowledge that we hold the reins of our life's wild ride is the empowering understanding that allows us to rest assured that the deeper meaning of our journey is in our hands. The key to a successful outing in the game of life is to grasp what is going on under the hood.

When we unveil the black box, we become the master of our own destiny. The ability to open our earthly eyes to the fact that our perceptions determine the reality of our choosing allows us to transcend the disconnection and fear that lies in that world that is not always completely of our design.

We are the architect, the artisan and the general contractor of our earthbound construction. Know well that life will create circumstances for our interaction and perseverance, and it is our gift to experience our days with grace and exuberance.

Learn from the opportunities as they are presented. They are all offered to us based on the manifestations of our design.

Be the acceptance that paves your way, be the one who lights the path, and be well!

Experiences, Extrapolations and Exultations

As we move through our lives, we have the opportunity to connect with fellow travelers sharing our experiences, extrapolations and exultations. These tangent points of intersection bring with them the occasion to gift warm wishes and kindness to the kindred spirits on our path.

The vibration you hold is easily transferred through interaction on any level. Collaboration ignites the forge of the universe to meld a higher frequency to receptive souls.

Please know that your empathy brings with it a heightened sense of universal compassion and well-being. Your benevolent efforts are a line in the cosmic script that we all draw from in the upper realm.

The journal scribed from our journey records intention and action. The law of attraction will manifest itself in the boomerang effect of your design.

Be the purveyor of kindness, be the recipient of goodness, and be well!

Outward Generosity Starts with Inner Compassion

From the time we are born into our earthly body to the time we retire its incarnation, we search, create and hope to embrace our true self. The essence we cling to in our lifetime may or may not be the personification of our true intent.

The journey we undertake is one that sees us through days with the hopeful belief that we can be true to our calling. The knowledge that the deepness of our soul is at our core is the grounding on which we can depend.

As our adventure unfolds based on our life plan and its supporting actions, we come to realize that we are the amalgamation of the kindness and energy we grant ourselves. The algorithm we design becomes the poetry of our consciousness.

When we raise above the fear that we may fall short of our mark, we learn to walk the steps of our days without concern or self-derision. The goals we set are a generous guideline and are never to be taken as fail proof.

The life we afford our being is the gift we grant to ourselves knowing well that you are the best self you can be. Outward generosity starts with inner compassion for the illumination of your heart's light.

Be the biggest fan of your self-identification, be the beacon you follow home, and be well!

Creature of Love

Love is the highest frequency we have the opportunity to align ourselves with on Earth. This pure vibration has the ability to cure the sick, soothe the masses and unite peoples.

Much of the manifested experience is fixated on control. Controlling production, wealth and even thought. This energetic wrestling match is a tug-of-war that depletes us if we allow it to become our perception.

By maintaining our connection with the higher source, we grant ourselves permission to maintain residence in the hallowed space. This knowledge allows us safe passage to travel from the manifested to the unmanifested and back again with ease.

Our round-trip voyage is by design our daily journey from the awake to the dream state where we replenish our physical body with ethereal light. Make every effort to be a creature of love and an emissary of kindness and joy!

Be at peace, be a catalyst for change, and be well!

More Than Our Self-Interest to Consider

We are born to our earthly incarnation with a purpose and an innate desire to achieve the goals we set out to accomplish. As we venture onward with our lives, we come to realize that there is more than just our self-interest to consider.

The transcendence we achieve is one that sees our ability to connect with something greater than ourselves. This connection we feel is Spirit and our essence's alignment to the universal energy that permeates us all.

As we continue to mature on our life's path, we are gifted this understanding with all of the joy and responsibility that comes with it. Know in your heart that your purpose is grand and that you have the ability to achieve beyond your wildest dreams.

Your unification with the source is as omnipresent as you allow it to be. Opening yourself at your core to this universal truth will empower your psyche and bring joy to your days.

Be the power you seek to manifest the reality you desire, be the sanctuary you require to feel safe and accomplished, and be well!

You Were Constructed for a Higher Purpose

The Now is the focal point of all time, space and reality. When we allow our attention to drift off into the past or the future, we diffuse our energy and limit our ability to receive.

Our openness to the universe's source code determines connection and productivity. A willingness to stay aligned to presence paves the way for creativity and abundance.

The frequency we attune our perception to is of our choosing. Higher vibrations create happiness and attract others in a similar state of consciousness.

Work hard to avoid worry, anger and fear; these low resonations weigh us down and inhibit our ability to rise above the issues that create the discourse in our lives. Know you were constructed for a higher purpose and allow your goodness to reign supreme.

Simply be, be happy, be present, and be well!

Inner Inventory

The biggest choice we face on a daily basis is how much love and kindness we wish to share with the world around us. We are all endowed with light within our soul's core and we have the opportunity to parse this gift as we see fit.

Some may covet this prize for themselves, while others may give all they have to their fellows. The action we take is the energy we emit in the governance of our karmic experience.

Please know that kindness works on a sliding scale, and we are never required to outlay more than we can afford at any given moment. It is our innate right to look inward at a first glance to determine our own needs before looking to spread seeds outwardly.

We all have requirements of our own, and they must be tended to before we look to our dependents to bolster their life force. This inner inventory should never be looked upon as selfish, as it is self-sustenance that maintains our personal well-being.

Know well that you have what you require and what remains is yours to do with as you see fit. Your plan of action is not static, nor is your ability, as your goals may change along with your journey.

Be the one who understands your inner responsibility, be the harvest as well as the shepherd, and be well!

Amazement Without Awe

Life on Earth is designed to test our limits. The environment was created to teach the greatest achievement of all, that of acceptance. As we progress on our journey, we encounter challenges and jubilation.

The tide of time teaches the passive participant that the experience will venture forward no matter their level of participation. The more attuned traveler learns quickly that the energy of the manifested realm is a powerful torrent that continuously flows towards the goal of growth physically, emotionally and spiritually.

As we gain our footing and elevate our vibration, we strive to build a tolerance to the negative attitudes that prevail in the lower frequencies. The prevalent understanding in the higher realms is that resistance to what is in the Now only drains the soul and depletes life force.

The full library of the universe's knowledge is available to those in the present moment. If we can stand back and learn to observe what life has to offer without assigning value or creating labels, one's connection to the unmanifested source code remains in full effect.

Be amazed without awe, be conscious without boundaries, and be well!

Strength of Mind

At our core, we know we possess the innate ability to access the knowledge we need to succeed. This inner guidance is the nurturing we learn to accept as we mature on our path.

The strength of mind we train ourselves to have is the gift we grant unto ourselves. These nutrients feed our soul and bolster our ability to master the lessons we have come here to learn.

Every experience we encounter was drawn to us by divine providence to enhance our foresight and better our station on our earthly journey. Please know this life of yours is full of purpose and meaning, all attuned to your higher calling.

Be kind to yourself, be your own silver lining, and be well!

What is Truly Important

Our lives have a purpose, and every goal we have ever set was designed with our best interest in our mind's eye. This axiom, being a hard fast truth, allows us to acknowledge that we work best in environments where we derive pleasure from the experience.

Happiness stems from a sense of security and a bi-directional exchange of positive energy. This alchemy creates a symbiosis between an individual and the universe, as one's self-worth increases in direct correlation with the level of satisfaction that is received from our daily existence.

We strive to create a level of contentment, and this is easier said than done if you have the manifested world's pressures on your shoulders. I humbly suggest that you step back and take an inventory of what is truly important to you.

Health, safety and security reign supreme; the rest is generally superfluous. Setting your priorities and output of energy to align with what makes you joyful will pave the way for positive results knowing in your heart what matters, and what matters will fill your heart.

Be aware of your energetic output, be mindful of the energy you absorb, and be well!

Believe in Your Path

The greatest challenge we all face every second of our lives is staying focused. The human mind tends to wander into the dark spaces that exist outside of our control.

We find that if we allow ourselves the grace of grounding found in the present moment, we are afforded a peace of mind in this residence. Looking backwards, or daydreaming forwards, leaves you powerless in the Now.

The only truth we can be sure of is what we know in presence. Work hard to manage your life force to align with your environment so you reap the universe's full benefit.

Trust in what you see. Believe in your path; walk it with your head raised high and intentions affixed to the goodness in your heart.

Be a courageous contributor to your life's plan, be safely at home where you stand, and be well!

Intention in Your Day

When you awoke this morning, did you have a plan? Did you set your intentions to manifest the day of your choosing?

As we map out the destination in our mind's eye, we require the clarity that only we can create for ourselves. Reverse engineering from the desired location or state of mind is the metaphysical push pin on the universe's map that starts the process.

Knowing is the anchor, and being is the action that allows the energy to come to you to manifest your choosing. Enlightenment is the passport you seek to anywhere in your imagination.

Be intentionally in how you approach your day, be open to what you draw to you, and be well!

All Things Become Possible

The only limitations are the ones we sadly place upon ourselves; there is no universal blueprint for what anyone can and cannot do. Once we open our mind to this freeing ideal, all things become possible.

The key is setting your intent and following the path that starts with a vision and leads to its desired outcome. This requires what some refer to as patience, but if you let go of your hopeful timeline, it will undoubtedly lead you to that exact spot you plotted on your life's roadmap.

Please know it's all working to plan and move through your days, knowing well your intent is in alignment with the goals. Work hard to create a synergy with the universe that allows the cosmic tumblers to align with your highest and best purpose.

There is no prescribed age, education or station in life that governs the ability to start the process. Freeing your mind and letting go is the gateway to transcendence.

Be above concern, be giving of your energy to those in need, and be well!

Mirror of Intentions

Our life experiences are a mirror of the intentions we set and the energy we hold true in our heart. Know well that we set the pace and create the circumstances for the peace of mind we seek.

Some choose to live life as if it were a constant fire drill, and others elevate their being to function in a space where they manage their reality with self-love and compassion. The choice is always ours based on our perceptions.

The ability to act rather than react allows us to reign over our creation with grace and understanding. We manifest the tempo of our journey based on our acceptance of the present moment's energetic output.

When we work with what we receive, we flow with the universe's intent and friction is eliminated. The lack of resistance to what is, opens the tumblers on the locks of the cosmos freeing symbiosis to lead the way.

Stress is merely a situation we have fed with the negative energy in which drama thrives. Raise your consciousness above the level of fear and anxiety by being one with what happens.

Be what you feel in your soul, be aligned unto your choosing, and be well!

Regain Your Complete Self

The essence of life is the magic that touches our physical and ethereal selves. This all-powerful force is the binding energy that creates the conduit between Heaven and Earth.

The love that is within us all empowers connection and positivity. This heavenly vibration attunes to the highest frequency and is readily available to all.

To reach the euphoric state of Buddhistic bliss, all one needs to do is remain present and accept what is; the tools are simple to use and at your fingertips. Open your soul to the possibilities that have been right in front of you from the start.

Embrace your inner child on a mission back to where you parted ways so long ago. You know the way; it's not far. In fact, stop thinking and seize the Now and regain your complete self!

Be loving, be present, and be well!

Transcend Earthly Confines

The awakening of the soul is the opening of the mind's eye to the understanding that purpose, being and action fall into alignment when left to follow the energetic path the universe sets forth. The knowing that there is always more than meets the eye is the sanctification that grounds our experience in deeper connection.

Life is a glorious ride, and its purpose is meant as one of growth, compassion and love. When we allow our essence to truly exist in a state of presence, we draw the power we need to transcend earthly confines.

Rise above the stress and anxiety that govern the lower realm of reality with a true belief that your path will be the one you seek. Avoid setting expectations for the journey you have before you.

Allow your travels to venture to the places unknown that call to your life purpose. Your teachers await you for the lessons you desire in your heart.

Be fluid in your beliefs of what is and what should be, be a conductor for passion and universal well-being, and be well!

Every Moment is a Gift

The "I am" in which your presence resides is the amalgamation of all you have experienced and the perceptions you have created. Know well that within this state of understanding lies the invisible couplings that tie you to the high space wherein there is no disconnection from kindness and love.

The energy that bonds the manifested framework to the universal source code works independently from any earthly timeline. The acceptance that your existence is a critical component in the grander scheme is a portal to deeper knowledge and enlightenment.

As we move through our journey, we may rest at ease that every moment has been a gift. The skills you have amassed and the relationships you have forged continue to be the blessings on your path that shine light on what greatness there is to come.

Be confident in your connections, be open to new blessings, and be well!

Your Purpose is Clear

Our lives are tailor made for personal growth. The opportunity for our emotional evolution is hardwired into the seams of the very fabric of our existence.

We wake as an infant clinging to every sound and vibration our surrounding offers as the stimuli we use to formulate our basis for perception. These sensory inputs are custom made for the path we have chosen to walk.

As we progress on our road, we encounter options that allow for the fine tuning that shapes our being as we mature. This metamorphosis is nurtured by the vastness of possibility and abounding energy that we have at our disposal.

Know in your heart that your purpose is as clear as you choose it to be, and your ability to fulfill it is always within your control. The rules of the game are yours for the design, and there is only one possible outcome, and that is one of success.

Be true to your master plan, be alive in your living, and be well!

Governing Properties

The manifested world in which we call home functions as an earthly overlay to the grander, unmanifested realm. This facade acts as a universal translator allowing all people attuned to a given vibratory frequency to share their realities within the earthbound experience.

The physical world is governed by properties that are distilled versions of overarching universal laws. The physics we are beholden to as residents and caretakers of this space creates a working set of tangible guidelines that can be read like an instruction book.

Knowing the rules allows us to become good stewards of our environment. The knowledge that we are here to learn and that lessons will repeat with accruing severity until acknowledged and put to use is the key to growth and prosperity.

Acceptance is the fulcrum for all working interactions on Earth. This opening of heart and soul leads to happiness and understanding.

When your thoughts and actions are in alignment with the energy at hand, things move without friction. Keeping the wheels moving and the tracks greased enhances your ability to move through life with relative ease and comfort.

Be one with what happens, be the facilitator of expansive action coupled with endearing kindness, and be well!

Unplug

Our immersion in our surroundings is the energetic conduit that stimulates harmonic conversion with the source vibrations of our choosing. The perception of our environment sets the stage for our state of mind and subsequent actions.

When we allow ourselves true disconnection with the noise of other's auric fields, we gain a deeper understanding of the data that is intended for our consumption without filter or distraction. The shortest path to the recommended solitude is best facilitated in the open space of nature.

The portal to oneness with creation is opened easily during what we refer to as a walking meditation. The opportunity to align your manifested body with your unmanifested higher-self beckons the source code you require for clarity and peace of mind.

Finding the time to unplug and just be will serve you well. Walk with an open mind and soul allowing the static to clear and your mindfulness to govern the experience.

Be aware of your ability to drawn from the universal foundation, be attuned to your purpose, and be well!

Attending the School of Life

As we sit firmly in the manifested space, with our feet on the ground and our eyes wandering from sight to sight, we gain perspective. The understanding of our presence is the portal to deeper connection and well-being.

Our days are chapters, and its pages are complete with the lessons we require. The vision we allow ourselves is based on the alignment to the frequency to which we attune.

The instruction is present for all who truly attend the school of life, and its abundance is aligned with our desired outcome. The home in which we live, the careers we have chosen and the company we keep are all the exhibition of our acceptance of the success criterion of our design.

Be the triumph in your life, be a purveyor of goodwill, and be well!

Ever-Adjusting Self-Illustration

Our experiential existence is, by design, a laboratory for alchemy. The experiences we encounter are test benches with no precalculated success criteria.

The interactions of our life are fluid without foregone pattern or destination. As we progress on our path we encounter inputs that shape the opinions that we base our foundational assumptions upon.

The baseline that we create is as personal as our thumbprint. The uniqueness that we manifest has no litmus test, no right or wrong, it simply is.

As one's tenure reaches a venerable state, an application of collected worldly comprehension sets our standards for perception, communication and action. This ever-adjusting self-illustration of how life should be becomes our calling card to the explicit surroundings in which we intend to coexist.

No matter the circumstances we face, there is, and was never any incorrect path to travel. Every decision and its subsequent actions have reaction and consequence with their assigned lessons to be learned.

Herein lies the ability to grow no matter which fork in the road is chosen. Some lessons come easy and others with trial and error; no matter the degree of resilience required, the bunny slopes of life will achieve education as well as the black diamond trails traveled.

Be open to the journey, be forgiving of yourself, and be well!

Shining Brightly

We are all attracted to energetic beings and experiences that resonate in vibratory fields similar to our own. This law of attraction is a core principle of universal mechanics.

Know well that we will beckon to us that which we emanate. As a simple rule of thumb, take great care in being a source of kindness, warmth and joy for the community in which you reside.

Open your heart and mind to the vast possibilities that are presented to you daily. The opportunity to shine brightly is a personal choice and an excellent alternative to other less brilliant options.

Be the one that others can count on, be a source of inspiration, and be well!

Utopian Equilibrium

The universe is based on a set of laws, and these principles govern mechanics at the quantum level. We work within the dynamics presented to us as an infallible baseline.

The language we all speak in our daily interactions is that of mathematics. The core functionally we are presented with at the programmatic level is intended to create a balance.

This utopian equilibrium is the fundamental homeostasis that nature works tirelessly to manifest. As we raise our awareness and vibrations increase, we see beyond what is presented to the naked eye.

The frequency we are gifted to align with is that which surpasses the balancing of the earthly formula as we strive for deeper synchronicity. Within the symphonic configuration lies that of an interrelated ecosystem where there is no disconnect between Heaven and Earth.

Some call it Heaven, some call it Buddhistic bliss, and the quantum physicists refer to it as the zero point field. This space contains the earthbound frequency in harmony with the upper realms that are best described in Chinese philosophy as the yin and yang of the universe.

Know well that our ultimate goal is to walk the halls of the highest conscious space with mindfulness. This hallowed opportunity is all of ours for the acceptance.

Be in blissful balance, be aligned with presence, and be well!

Assessing for Risk and Benefit

As we walk life's path, we are gifted with opportunities to make choices that determine situational outcomes and formulate our perceptions. The decisions we make are based on our experiential knowledge and the goals we have to achieve.

We exist in a constant state of assessing our surroundings for risk and benefit. This assessment process is one that requires vigilance and perseverance to establish the appropriate response.

Once we have ascertained that a given energetic variable poses a threat to our well-being, the path of least resistance is to mitigate exposure to the offending factor. Knowing well that not all challenges can be avoided, this process is one that requires a personal ranking system that allows for a variance based on both internal and external factors.

The encouraged goal before us all is to live a productive and happy life free of fear, anger and negativity. If we incorporate the policy that poking the bear is generally not the best course of action, we will thrive in a relatively trouble-free existence.

Be aware that actions have consequences, be mindful of your intent, and be well!

Your Personal Hero's Journey

We all come into the world with innate talents to be shared. The manifestation of these gifts may present themselves at an early age, or they may come to light as we mature.

The acceptance of ourselves as who we are is the first step in gaining the personal awareness necessary to flourish. The fortitude we find within is the anchor point we springboard from to connect to the world around us.

As we learn to receive the power of our individual strength, we look to our manifested knowledge base and the real-time information we receive from the source to move us along our path. As our vibration increases, our frequency aligns to the higher space where we realize the infinite possibilities that lay before us.

Our lives are of our making and the experience is uniquely individual to behold. Know well that you are earmarked for the expedition that suits your life purpose and the adventure is your personal hero's journey.

Be the steward of your talents, be extraordinary in your pursuits, and be well!

What Truly Matters

Our eyes are the gateway to our soul and we must maintain this sacred portal with great care and compassion. As we walk the Earth, we have the opportunity to bring our innate heavenly understanding into our incarnation.

As we gaze upon the world through the lens we create, we are gifted the ability to choose our thoughts and the vibrations they manifest. The acceptance of love as your baseline energetic emanation elevates your frequency to an attunement where laughter prevails over sadness and kindness quells fear.

We are here to help. We are here to aid our fellow travelers on their journey as well as lift ourselves up to the heights we seek in our mind's eye.

Take the time to assess what truly matters. This purposeful evaluation will shed light on what lies before you and will grant you the foresight to smile and simply laugh.

Be the joy on your path, be light on the way, and be well!

Introspection is the Foundation

If you step back and ask yourself why you are here, you will most likely generate a long list of answers. Upon closer inspection, the odds are very high that the replies you produce are more likely additional questions than the resolutions you thought you were seeking.

The ability to access your personal blueprint is one that comes on the road to enlightenment. Introspection is the foundation for the illumination that lights the pages of our self-designed manuscript.

The adventure we all set out to embrace is one that we create in our mind's eye to fulfill our deep-rooted need to expand our awareness and connection. This journey is the heroic purpose of our time spent as a traveler.

Be considerate to yourself, be compassionate to others, and be well!

No Moment is Wasted

Take a deep breath, exhale and repeat the process a few times until you feel a sense of calm as the external melts away. Use this inner marker to stake a place in your soul space that allows you freedom and peace.

Our daily routines very seldomly leave any time to simply be, and this erodes our foundational need to connect to that natural environment in which we reside. When we open our mindset to the productivity that manifests in the nothingness, we broaden our scope of understanding to include the stillness as oneness.

When we plug into the flow of the universe, we come to the awareness that no moment is wasted. That there is no second of time that is not being put to good use.

There is benefit to all interaction, and the when necessary, inaction. As we wait, we take the required pause to allow our essence to absorb the goodness that nurtures the experience.

Grant yourself the latitude to rest your mind and body. This cessation of movement and thought allows for the necessary syncing of your psyche with your life's plan as you download its data from the source.

Be the intermission that beckons in health and prosperity, be the smile that arises from your earthly interlude, and be well!

Our Earthly Baseline

The universe in which we live is a system of interconnection and energetic symbiosis. This skillfully designed framework houses the dendrites that stimulate interaction and perception.

If we were able to recall our time in-utero, we all plugged into the docking mechanism that directly receives knowledge from the source. As we developed in the womb, we began to take on the earthly stimuli from our surroundings.

The externality of these early inputs sets the foundation for the journey to come. As we mature, the mingling of our innate knowledge with what we learn to perceive becomes our earthly baseline for understanding.

True success comes when a grounding occurs that allows your hardwired firmware to work in concert with the path you walk and the lessons you learn. Know well that you were born with the tools you need and the gifts you have to apply them.

The mastery we all strive for is that in which our sense of being intertwines with our deeper knowledge and connection to the cosmos. Herein lies the true path to understanding.

Be ethereal in spirit, be grounded in action, and be well!

Who We Choose to Be

We all have a deep-rooted desire to understand the world in which we live. We work tirelessly from the time we are children to get our arms around our surroundings as best we can to feel connected and in tune.

As we mature, we begin to realize that our environment is a mirror of our perceptions, and it's best seen when our vision of our inner self is clearly portrayed outwardly. The grounding we seek externally can only be achieved when we make the decision on who we choose to be in our own space.

Your inner self is not meant to be a static creation, and may morph as often as you like. Rest well knowing that you are who you make your mind up to be and that your life's path and all of the supporting experiences will change along with the self you present.

All you need to do is fully accept your creation, and your masterpiece will draw to it the energy, people and outcomes that work to your highest and best purpose. Being the best you is easily achieved when you eliminate any expectations and simply live your life with passion, kindness and intent.

Be content with who you are, be kind to yourself, and others and be well!

Nurture Your Desired State

We are taught to chase what we desire to make our dreams come true. Please consider that the energy you spend on this pursuit may be ill-placed.

When we focus on the hunt, we lose sight of the prize. The intention of life is to learn, love and grow through experience.

The opportunity to manifest our vision is a hardwired ability. The unearthly firmware that exists within us can only be accessed when we transcend and allow presence to permeate our being.

Attention to the Now creates the energetic space that nurtures our desired state and this welcoming force of light is the beacon that attracts and sustains goodness and joy. Through this portal, we achieve personal happiness while welcoming others to follow in our path.

Be still, be a gatekeeper for kindness and joy, and be well!

Free Will

We are all products of our environment. The growth process we undertake from our earthly birth to heavenly ascension is a coupling of our innate knowledge with the lessons we learn.

The study of nature verses nurture is a fascinating discussion that generally omits one critical variable, that of free will. We all have certain predispositions based on our genetics, and this hardwiring is truly affected by the environment in which we are raised, but please know well that we always play an active role in who we become.

Some choose to live life on autopilot and mimic the paths of their parents without straying far from what they were taught or even held dear as youngsters. Others venture outward, breaking the mold, thus proving that the apple can fall, and even roll as far away from the tree as it wishes.

We are who we desire to be. The opportunity is omnipresent and the joy of self is yours for the making based on the vision you have for your existence.

Be fully invested in who you are, be the pronouncement of your assertion of freedom of self-expression, and be well!

Connecting with Goodness

The connection we create with our fellows is the reference point we fall back on to set our baseline. This starting point is the fulcrum we use to leverage our position both energetically and pragmatically.

The decision we make to attune our life frequency to a positive vibration sets the stage for our ensuing interactions. When we allow our focus to be in the present moment, we connect with the goodness that the universe has to bestow upon us.

The resonate energetic band we align to can be a constant or a variable; the opportunity is yours to fix or fluctuate as you see fit. The goal is to create an environment in which you can best absorb the life lessons as they present themselves to you on your path.

Allow yourself the opportunity to accomplish the goals in your mind's eye without undue stress or pressure. Know that your presence is what is required and your kindness to yourself and others is the fuel that stokes the fires of motivation and accomplishment.

Be kind, be the warrior of your heart's message, and be well!

Through Simplicity

The experiences we call life are a compilation of the lessons we set forth to learn. This path we walk is best realized as the action we call to us by design.

As we grow and mature, we come to the realization that we reap what we sow, and all outcomes bolster our knowing and aid in forming our future perspective. The frequency of our choosing ebbs and flows based on our energetic alignment.

The depth we seek is readily available to us once we grant ourselves access to a joyful existence. Through the simplicity we maintain in our being, we pave the road we wish to travel.

Living a mindful existence minimizing pollutants aligns you with Spirit. Know well that toxicity comes to us though negative thought, action, surroundings and unnatural food/drink.

Work hard to purify your being. The cleaner you live, the happier you will be.

Be aware of your needs, be aligned with what is truly best for your mind, body and soul, and be well!

Contentment's Litmus Test

Very few of us were blessed to come into this world with a clear recollection of exactly why we are here. You can take solace in the fact that our life's ambitions may very well be moving targets that we set, reset and then set again.

The growth we experience on our journey comes to us as we interact on the path of our choosing. The roads we travel are the mapped courses we set to guide us to the destinations we have in our mind's eye.

The end points we seek are the culmination of our perceptions, and these desires are therefore manifestations of what we deem as necessary for our happiness and prosperity. The success criteria we set is never in stone and the litmus test that proves our contentment is based on a sliding scale that is altered by necessity and station in life.

Know well that yesterday's goal easily become today's old news as our view of our needs takes on new light with our updated life condition. We chase what we feel we need, while in reality we need to feel what we require.

To garner true grounding, safety and security, we must look past the sparkly objects that catch our momentary attention. The knowledge of who you are and why you are here is the divining rod to attract and build upon the energy that is here to sustain us all.

Be more than what meets the eye, be a light for others by recognizing your purpose, and be well!

Balancing Perspective

Happiness is the state of mind emanating from within when we grant ourselves true acceptance. Learning to release control opens our experience to the possibilities of the stimuli that surrounds us.

Know in your heart that the adventure we are all on is a tale destined for growth and mindful expansion. It is our personal responsibility to raise our awareness to understand that life is a process and the journey will teach us the skills we require to balance the perspective gained from both positive and negative outcomes.

As we mature, we come to the reckoning that there is as much to learn from failure as there is victory. Without the darkness, we would never understand the power of the light.

It is beyond our scope to control the sands of time; what is within our domain is our free will to decide what we feel about the experience as it presents itself. Know in your soul that your alignment with optimism will always fill your heart with joy, and this vibration will attract more of the same in proliferation.

Be the source of your own smile, be the creator of the positivity that lights your way, and be well!

Metaphysical Pie Chart

Life teaches us that we reap the benefits of the lessons learned as the result of our attention. We are the amalgamation of our thoughts, actions and their resulting outcomes.

The metaphysical pie chart we create as we allocate our focus is a work in progress that is adjusted based on our changing agenda and goals. The mastery we strive to achieve has its underpinnings in the level of energy we are able to exude.

The frequency that we align our output to is the resonate channel that we also tune into to draw our power. This bi-directional exchange is one that connects actions with outcomes through a symbiotic process.

This symbiosis is the bridge that is the catalyst for the energies manifested on Earth to merge with those from the higher plain. The unmanifested upper floors house the deeper connection that is steeped in love, light and joy.

Early on in childhood, we innately reside in the unmanifested space. As we progress linearly in the manifested realm, we encounter occasions that lower our vibration through concern and even trauma.

These trigger points create karmic scar tissue that reroutes thought processes and energetic well-being. The secret to staying young of heart is to make the conscious choice to reside in the higher frequency's penthouse to enjoy the view of your choosing and creation.

Be enthusiastic in your endeavors, be aligned with the light, and be well!

Keeping Life in Perspective

Our life is as calm or chaotic as we desire it to be based on our perceptions. The waves of time and energy do not stop, or even slow, for any set of earthly circumstances.

It is our responsibility to ourselves and our surroundings to manage not just our expectations, but our reactions to what comes to us on our path.

Know well that you have complete control your perspective at all times. The expertise you have honed and nurtured to this point has gifted you the skills to ride the waves with grace.

Look deep within yourself to keep life's experiences in proportion to living the way that is truly in alignment with you higher purpose. There will always be things happening and people coming and going, but what stays constant is your view of your own reality.

Be the anchor point you depend on for your own well-being, be the port in the storm for others to rely on, and be well!

Sandbox of Our Soul

From our earliest recollections, we have looked in the mirror and pondered. This deep introspection became, and may very well remain, the anchor point of our being when all of the pretense in our lives melts away and we stare naked into the core of our existence.

The self-awareness granted in refection is our gift unto ourselves. This unencumbered safe space is the sandbox of our soul.

Within this environment, we allow ourselves the honesty to evaluate our purpose, our actions and our deeper connections. Life, the universe, and our place in it is an omnipresent puzzle with its pieces in constant flux.

Our paths intersect with opportunity and like travelers on similar journeys. When we welcome in our experiences and our compatriots with open arms, we prime the pump for the energetic flow that fulfills our purpose and solves the questions we lay before ourselves.

Know well who you are as a person of skill, empathy and desire. Acceptance of your character and station is paramount to the ability to self-soothe and create abundance.

Be kind to yourself, be patient with your journey, and be well!

Superpowers

We all have special abilities, and these superpowers are the gift we are here to share with the world. As we mature, we learn to open ourselves to the unknown through the acceptance that there is much more than we initially understood at first glance.

As we encounter what life has to offer, we elevate our attunement to new frequencies that open our travels to the vast array of people, places and lessons here for us to experience. The growth that is offered to us is as grand in scope as we wish to receive.

Know in your heart that your willingness to simply participate in the newness that abounds is the catalyst for the expansion of your mind and soul. Every morning awakens to the possibility of a deeper understanding of your life's path and the joy that is yours to embrace through its creation.

Be thirstful for newness, be accepting of what is offered, and be well!

Gaining Mastery

We all gravitate to what we know and makes us feel safe. This feeling of safety is the security that allows for our repetition of action and the residual benefits that arise as we gain mastery.

The actions that make up our days range from routine to the exhilarating, but please know all are sacrosanct in their being. Every moment is an opportunity to learn, share and grow.

As we rise above the feeling that some parts of our existence are perfunctory, we gain the perspective that can only be seen from on high. This sense of grounding allows for the assignment of joy to be shared in all aspects of our lives.

Know well that the opportunity is yours to not just live, but to be alive; breathe in the fresh air, hug your loved ones and share your enjoyment of being. There are no limits on the amount of happiness you can manifest and propagate to the world.

Be alive in your being, be a catalyst for joy, and be well!

Making Our Mark

We've all come here with a purpose. This calling may be as grand or as understated as we so choose.

As we experience our days, we share our essence with all we are blessed to encounter. The vibration we emanate is intended to enhance our environment and its foundational framework.

The responsibility we all have is to make our mark. The indelible etching we manifest is our personal contribution and gift to be cherish.

Look deep within to bring your life plan to its fruition here on Earth. Your path will intertwine with all that your heart brings to reality.

Be bold, be the spirit within, and be well!

Providing Guidance, Calm and Connection

We were born with a purpose, a plan, and the means to accomplish what we set out to achieve. The key to success is acceptance, a true letting go of what you perceive as what should be and the ability to work with the actual reality of the situation at hand.

Your knowledge and understanding of the bigger picture will allow for a higher-level perspective to drive your actions and their outcomes. This enlightened viewpoint is one that opens the portal to the source energy that flows to you as needed and provides guidance, calm and connection.

Be open to receive, be in alignment with what is sent to you, and be well!

Our Soulful Psyche

We live our lives in search of happiness, and the reality is we need look no farther than the mirror to manifest the internal kindness found in self-consciousness. The knowledge that we create our own experience is the grounding we can always depend on to elevate our vibration to a healthy space.

Our earthly mind and body rely on the messages they receive from our soulful psyche to determine their course of action. The reliance on the mood set by perception dictates our reactions to the stimuli presented on our journey.

As we travel our life's course, we will undoubtedly hit bumps along the way. These are all opportunities to gain a refreshed vantage point to foster growth.

Know in your heart that you will be presented the awareness you require to build the health and happiness you seek. Gaze inward to reflect on your path to draw the strength you need to elevate yourself to the level of you choosing.

Be the alchemist of your enlightenment, be the master of your own mental and physical well-being, and be well!

Heights of Possibility

Life is a classroom meant for the expansion of our knowledge while deepening our understanding and broadening our connection. The success of any educational endeavor is measured in its retention and the application of the skills honed to daily use.

As we walk our paths, we build the curriculum of our existence. This moment-to-moment experience manifests the building blocks that we climb upon to see the heights of possibility.

As we ascend to new levels, our past knowledge base thins, and we may feel unprotected in the wake of the new data that lays before us. This freshness brings with it an air of vast potential.

The newness of this energy's power is to be embraced in the highest of space you intended it to be received. The frequency of your mindset is the key to your success.

Aligning your being with a highest of vibrations will open you to receive. Know well that you are exactly where you are meant to be to glean the lessons you require to maximize your potential and take full advantage of your possibilities.

Be above concern, be open to scholarship, and be well!

Life's Artistic Collection

As we grow, we learn to look at ourselves as a reflection of our perceptions. This inner awareness is something that we master as we participate in what life has to offer.

Our daily experience is crafted as the earthly incarnation of our life plan. Know well that as you look deeper into what you feel, you gain perspective on the depth of your soul.

The attachments you have are the manifestations of your grander understanding of the path you have paved. Looking upon yourself with kindness and compassion will open your heart to receive all that it requires for its expansion and transcendence.

Be the curator of your life's artistic collection, be gentle with your being, and be well!

Karmic Recruiting

Throughout our lives, we have the great honor of constructing the team we know to be true to a mutual cause. The lineup we amass is one that builds a consensus of energy, ability and desire to accomplish the goals at hand.

The quests your fellowship encounters are the like bonds that see you from one chapter to the next. This commonality of experience is the shared database that you all draw from as your baseline for understanding and application.

The collective encounters of your explorations builds your knowledge base as well as attracts new applicants to the corps. This karmic recruiting enhances the breadth of manifested and unmanifested wealth through the associations made on the journey.

The ever-expanding scope of high vibrating energies opens the communal portal for growth and deeper connection. The acceptance of, and association to your flock, is the catalyst for the greatest learning adventures of your life!

Be courageous, be true, and be well!

Our Caring Cohort

Life is a concert to be experienced as a member of the world's grand symphony. As we practice the roles we play for the solo pieces we are gifted to share with our earthly audience, we are supported by those in a similar resonate vibration.

These like-minded souls are those we are blessed to call friends. The love and support that we share with our caring cohorts transcends reason as its roots are deeper than manifested understanding.

The path we walk is never lonely if we are open to the kindness shared at the level of frequency in which we reside. Our tribe surrounds us with the warmth and compassion we require to grant our soul's safety and security.

Know well that you are part of something larger than yourself. Your connection to the universe is multifaceted and as strong as your embrace will allow.

Be in tune with your kinfolk, be the simplicity that beckons others to your side, and be well!

Introspection and Deeper Application

While necessity is undoubtedly the mother of all invention, it is also the platform by which we derive the deepest of understanding. Our life's purpose is omnipresent on our path, and its lessons present themselves at every turn.

Our level of awareness of the teachings as they cross our path is the variable. The instruction will never cease; it will in fact intensify if the messages go unheeded.

Taking inventory of your journey's manifested experiences is a wise practice. The acceptance of what your universal lesson has plan laid before you will create introspection and a deeper application for the fruits of the expedition's labors.

Be conscious of what you have overcome, be present with who it has allowed you to become, and be well!

Gifting the Sands of Time

The interaction we experience through our connection to our fellows is one that allows us to hone our patience and compassion. Gifting the sands of time the serenity to flow at their own pace fosters growth and maturity.

As we walk our path, we are blessed to nurture our tribe with wisdom, love and the space needed to flourish. As we blossom into the spirit we have envisioned, we share our energetic space with others in our purview.

The gestation period of a soul varies from incarnation to incarnation. We must take great care to create the necessary development framework required to embody the love of the universe in each and every traveler we meet along their journey.

Know in your heart that your path is yours to design, and your collaboration with others in a similar vibration brings with it the appropriate nourishment and shelter required. Your presence is the light of karmic enrichment that illuminates the way for the collective deeper understanding.

Be patient with yourself and others, be the watcher as life unfolds before your eyes, and be well!

The Empathetic Agreement

It's safe to say that the majority of us were taught from earlier childhood to do the best we could at everything we set out to accomplish, and that's all anyone can expect of us. While this axiom reigns true, we must never lose sight of the fact that we must include ourselves in the scope of this understanding.

Too often, we are our own harshest critic, and through that personal scrutiny we manifest self-induced pressure. The burden we unwittingly create for ourselves is one that is pointlessly limiting and counterproductive.

When we come to the empathetic agreement with our life's purpose that we are here to learn and part of learning is trial and error, we rise above the fear of failure. Allowing this weight to be lifted creates the space for creativity and joy to become the overarching theme of our existence.

Wearing a serious face from morning until night does not create productivity; it actually hampers the light from shining on us. This limitation shrouds our ability to connect to the happiness and love that surrounds us all.

Rise above the fear that you are not worthy. Know in your heart that none of this is meant to break you; its goal is to enhance your being though the vast set of experiences you draw toward you.

Be playful as you live, be aware of your strengths, and be well!

Familiarity, Trust and Confidence

Our friends are the group of our creation. Nothing can ever replace the dynamic that exists with our biological family, but the extension of warmth, love and understanding that envelops our lives from the meaningful relationships of our choosing is the catalyst for our growth and success.

We all measure our personal wealth by the litmus test of our design. There are clear ways to quantify financial success, but nothing is more powerful that the qualified symbiosis of true friendship.

This deep devotion is one that transcends the constructs of the relationship's original design. A true bond is one that is created with a tolerance built into the process for metamorphosis.

As we expand ourselves through experience, our friends have the opportunity to accompany us on our path. The ability to manifest long lasting relationships is a great gift.

We are blessed to have friends, and even more blessed in a hallowed space to retain them. The team we consciously build grows stronger over time through the familiarity, trust and the confidence we place in these roots.

Be nurturing to the collective, be charitable to your own design, and be well!

The Daily Decision

Every morning when we awake, we are faced with a decision. This daily inquiry is one that looks to us to decide what frequency we are planning to tune into for the day's events.

The choice is ours as far as where we align our vibration. Like presets on a radio, we fine tune our personal experience to the resonate level that suits us.

This process is one that is triggered by our thoughts and actions. When we overtly make the pronouncement that we will be aligning our energies to a positive channel, the higher realm's portal is opened.

From this deliberately positive starting point, we have the ability to hone in to adjust our purpose to the granular level of our specific intentions. The focus we create is the manifestation of the vision in our mind's eye.

Know well that you have connection to the deeper source, and this database is at your disposal with its information on standby for your customization. Your well-being and sense of purpose emanates from the universal access you grant yourself to the data at hand.

Be resolute in your self-care, be confident in your cause, and be well!

Our Quiver of Lessons Learned

As we mature, we expand our vison of the lay of the land and deepen our understanding of the rules of the game. The venerability we amass is the gift presented by the time served in the training ground of life.

Every experience brings with it a sharpening of wit and another arrow we can place in our quiver of a lesson learned. These stored tools are all readily accessible for application to a scenario yet to be manifested.

Gray hair is a badge of honor and a distinction to be cherished. Know well that your path has been one that has allowed you to become who you have chosen to be.

As we have ascended, we have bridged the understanding that was clouded by inexperience. The space that comprehension occupies is that of confidence and clarity.

Be proud of your accomplishments, be content in the space you sit, and be well!

The Face of the Undiscovered

Our lives are personal masterpieces of our own design and construction. Starting from as far back as you remember, and even farther, you have been on a mission.

This journey is one that consistently puts us in positions of introspection and wonder. The acceptance that life goals are set, expanded upon and then reset allows for the fluidity required for the magic to transcend time and space.

This moving target is one that has no destination or finality. The beauty of the experience is the ride itself.

The course changes with perspective, desire and resources. The map's plotting points are never in stone and you have the enchantment within you to own the helm of your voyage.

Know well that you maintain full control at all times. The responsibility is yours to grant yourself the kindness and understanding to allow ambiguity to be the guiding light that illuminates the path.

Be brave in the face of the undiscovered, be your own source of creation, and be well!

Mastery of Perspective

The universe is a cosmic web of interaction and outcome. There is a logarithmic effect that occurs with every new variable introduced to the equation.

As stewards of the process, the responsibility lays firmly on us to care for the environment while tuned to a positive frequency, thus allowing the manifestation of our thoughts and actions to propagate the same optimism and tranquility.

Know well that the seeds we plant will be the harvest of our choosing. Take great care to build the world that you wish to inhabit and share with those you love.

Be the master of your perspective, be the joy in your life, and be well!

Discriminating Dissemination

The universe in which we live was constructed as the training ground for our experiential growth through the exchange of energies and ideals. This interconnected symbiosis is the fiber that bonds and the oil that represses the friction of millions of moving parts.

As we move throughout our lifetime, we build a network based on camaraderie and common goals. This platform is multidimensional and shared with the souls you embrace.

Know well that your purpose is of your making, and that your ability to enhance the life of others is the gift granted unto you for your discriminating dissemination. Trust in your vision and Spirit will act as your guide.

Be part of the whole, be clear in your purpose, and be well!

Walk Confidently

Life's journey is a puzzle to be solved, a riddle to be answered, a game to be played and a joy to be shared! As we travel, we gain experience, and as we are immersed in our findings, we expand our very being through trust and interaction.

The broadening of our purview rewrites the very DNA we manifest and share with our bloodline. The world in which we exist is a playground that contains the insights required for our introspection and transcendence.

Our depth is limitless and ability to receive unbounded. Your perception is the portal.

The door is open for you to take a peek or confidently walk through. There is no time limit; you get as many shots at making sense of it all as you require.

Please know it's all here; have faith in yourself so you can elevate your game and see it all through your own lenses. Outstretch your hand if you need support.

You are never alone; please know this in your very being. You have your teammates all around you to pick you up, toss you the ball and watch your blind side while you make sense of it all.

Be in the game, be in tune with what surrounds you, and be well!

A Thought for Simple Being

The sun comes up and the sun goes down; everything in between is a blessing to be held in reverence. The outlook that life is a gift to be lived to its fullest is one that creates moments to be cherished.

It is abundantly clear that there is nothing ordinary. It's all magic to be soaked in, shared and expanded upon to raise the vibration of the auric circles in which we coexist.

Being aware of your aliveness tells your family and friends how much you care. Being unguarded with your feelings reaps the benefits that will come back to your open heart.

Be alive, be grateful for your sense of compassion, and be well!

Look Beyond What Should Scare You

Life has no guarantees; in fact, it's a play-at-your-own-risk pastime. Truth be told, its opportunity to elevate your understanding and awareness to the heights of mastery is unrivaled.

When we are able to embrace the fact that our very existence is a tightrope walk, we rise above the fear that has the power to paralyze the strongest heart and mind. Letting go is the gateway to life beyond limitation and the launching of infinite possibility.

Looking beyond what you were told should scare you and set your vision on what exhilarates you. Being the catalyst of your own potential is the dowry that was created to ensure your marriage to a deeper understanding of what's best for you and your tribe.

Be fearless, be unconquerable, and be well!

Karmic Algebra

Our path is our own unique journey that allows us to learn, cultivate our senses and master the art of expression. This personal experience is one that hones our skills and fosters connection with oneness beckoning in the deeper source.

As we walk the earth, we observe and expand our understanding by incorporating what we see and accept as the way we wish to be received. This selection process is constantly evolving and never without new input to be assimilated.

The karmic algebra equation under consideration is by your design. The variables are your observations and you are the constant.

The balancing act is yours to manage as you measure the viability of the components you plug in for calculation. Receive well what is shared with you as it's meant to reinforce what you have previously extrapolated, knowing well that every contribution is valuable and holds profound meaning in its own right.

Be a cosmic mathematician, be inquisitive as well as observant, and be well!

Your Inner Barometer

The focus of our lives is to build ourselves into the humans we set forth to be. Know well that your character is the opus of your mind's eye.

There is no earthly design on your being. The individuality you create is contingent on the manifestation of your life plan.

Know well that there is no tangible measure on the rightness you achieve. Your own inner barometer is your measure of what fills your soul.

When we step back and take our personal inventory, we truly see the levels which we have achieved. The bar we set is ours and ours alone to measure the contentment we know within our hearts.

Be sanctified in your creation, be at peace with who you choose to be, and be well!

In Service to Your Highest and Best Purpose

Our lives are blank canvases for us to color as we like. The opportunities and possibilities are endless.

The one thing we can all be sure of is the fact that every situation is unique to our circumstances, and this customization will fit us like a glove. We know in our hearts that the lessons that we draw to us are based on our need to learn and grow as we experience what the curriculum has in store.

There are always options on how we apply what we glean even for the most rudimentary teachings. We can color within the lines or step outside the prescribed guidelines to create the masterpiece in our mind's eye.

There is no right or wrong, simply your personal application of how to use the tools imparted to you. The instructors employed in life's school will bring with them their own lesson plans and step-by-step how-to rules to achieve the goals at hand.

These may be portrayed to you as hard and fast parameters, when in reality any professor who tells you there is only one way to do anything is limiting your purview and inhibiting your ability to create a process of your own that fulfills your need to explore the possibilities of success and failure. Know well that tabula rasa is a beautiful starting point and that your imagination, courage and hard work will kindle the artwork for your personal gallery collection.

Admission is free to all who you welcome in from your circle of trusted friends, colleagues and advisors. The team is yours to build and this family unit will serve you and the collective well.

Be unattached to outcomes, be ok with what comes next, and be well!

Sharing Experiences and Wisdom

One of the greatest honors we have in life is the opportunity to share our experiences and the wisdom we have learned along the way. As others grant us the tribute of their attention, we are reciprocally blessed to learn from their goodwill and compassion.

The knowledge we gift is our reflections brought to light and utilized in presence. As we connect, we grow, and it is through this growth we expand our well-being and that of the collective.

Every day brings with it the possibility to better ourselves through the newness an open mind allows. Look at every situation with the eagerness of a child and the world will reward your enthusiasm with enlightenment and joy.

Be the teacher that calls to your inner knowing, be the student that fulfills your life purpose, and be well!

Puzzle Pieces

We all come here with gifts to share. Some of us have overt talents that are grandiose for all the world to recognize, while other special aptitudes are more internal and require a deeper introspective to identify.

No matter the level of our unique expressions, the world is blessed to have us all here to collaborate. The tools that we are all given are all pieces of a huge puzzle that was created to stimulate interaction through communication and cooperation.

The goal laid before all of us is to transcend the self and connect with the oneness that is omnipresent. The all-prevailing energy source is the constant that is the pictorial representation that the puzzle pieces interwoven when understood.

Embracing your abilities as the specialist you are is the first step in expanding your infinite possibilities. Step two is as simple as being open to what your heightened sense of awareness beckons into your life.

Be great at what you love, be loved for being great, and be well!

The Empathy You Feel for Others

As part of a collective community, we are charged with the omnipresent tasks of interaction, communication and collaboration. When these pillars of society are nurtured, a healthy environment is established and maintained for the well-being of its denizens.

The foundational thread that holds any group together is that of empathy for your fellows. The understanding you show for your comrade's situation in life is the bridge we build from one soul to another.

When we grant ourselves the space to rise above our own condition and employ the understanding that we are only part of a whole, we gain a perspective that allows for a deeper being. This acceptance of the magnitude of life brings with it a calm that arises when we lift the pressure from ourselves.

We are never the end all be all in any environment, we are simply a part of the magic that makes it all happen. Letting go of the do-or-die mentality opens your mindset to receive the energy that awaits you when you plug into the universal source.

Know in your heart that your feelings are your connection to the world around you. The sympathy you feel for others is the strength you are gifted with to draw enlightenment from on high and channel your energies to push forward the positive agenda you have in your mind's eye for yourself and the greater good.

Be aligned with what is, be part of what you know to be kindness and compassion, and be well!

Intentions and Actions

Our lives are the combined manifestations of our intentions and actions. The steps we take to bring our dreams to reality are always under our control.

Setting your mind's eye on what you envision makes you the champion of your own destiny. There is no one who understands your plan at a deeper level than you do, and there is no time like the present to settle into the role that allows you complete control of your life's purpose, direction and outcome.

The tools are at your disposal; through clearly charting your desired results, a path can be created. Simple activities like journaling, vision boarding, outlining, visualization, meditation and enlisting the input of trusted advisors can open the doors that you create in your visions.

Be clear in your intentions, be open to your personal power, and be well!

Bring Your Smile

Within us all we have the capacity to share and receive the energy that aligns with our chosen frequency. The vibration we emanate is the flag we wave to our environment stating our general intent.

We always have the opportunity to connect with our fellows as we build bridges and welcome the kindness of others into our lives. The world was created for our participation and collaboration to elevate the collective we share.

Look no farther than the space you inhabit to realize your full potential to make a difference. The life you live is a gift and the opportunity to flourish is yours for the making.

Bringing your smile and laughter to any situation is the grandest of contributions. When you spread your goodwill, you enhance the landscape and cultivate the field for others to harvest your compassion.

Be the plus-one on the invitation for life's party, be ever-present with your positivity, and be well!

The Cosmic Switchboard

Life may appear to be a linear progression of events that brings with it the feeling of endlessness. If you step back and elevate above the individual happenings, you can see the connectedness of it all.

When your focus becomes the present moment, it's all clear. The process is anything but linear; it's a waterfall decision tree that interconnects the universe's spiderweb-like connective tissue.

As we complete a goal, our attitude and presence of mind guide us to the next page of our self-written journey. Cognizance guarantees us the overview we seek to make the decisions and create the liaisons that patch us into the cosmic switchboard.

Interconnection transcends time and space. This magic fosters creativity, compassion and teamwork.

Be at peace with what happens, be on board with the plan of your creation, and be well!

Essence Radiates Intent

The greatest blessing we have is the love we share with our friends and family. The bonds we create are the connections that ground and sustain us.

The knowledge that we are never alone is what bolsters our being, and grants us the strength and courage we need to accomplish the goals we have in our mind's eye.

The opportunity to share our feelings with those we cherish is a gift that never tires or wears thin. Seize every chance you get to share your admiration, love and appreciation.

There can never be too much when it comes to feelings of the heart. Know well that your essence radiates your intent, and your kindness and compassion will always be well received and reciprocated by those enveloped by your caring embrace.

Be open with your feelings, be generous with your energy, and be well!

Moving From One Truth to the Next

Our word is our audible signature, and the frequency it carries attracts responses with a similar vibration. The resonate field that we create with our intention to communicate or deceive is clearly imprinted in our autograph.

The truth travels in the highest of spaces, and it is received well by all to whom it is imparted. When we offer reality to others, they return in kind, and its benefits are shared by all involved.

The use of anything less than the truth creates a shift in the communication paradigm and a breach is created. This gap in realism generates an alternate state of being that is stationed in a lower vibration and attracts a negative form of response.

This alternate lessor understanding of the event's chronicles manifests confusion, disconnection and possibly fear. The simplest way to maintain a firm handle on the transcripts of our lives is to maintain one single thread of reality.

This simple truth is that the ease in doing business we all strive for in our work and personal lives is holding fast to what we know as our grounding in reality. As the shortest distance between two points is a straight line, the simplest way to live your life is moving from one truth to the next.

Be aligned with actuality, be clear and precise in your communications, and be well!

Your Thought's Intentions

We are the culmination of our energetic intent. The time we spend in ponderance of our next thought or action are the seeds we scatter to the winds of our mind's eye.

Our lives are the perpetual harvest of our culminating endeavors. As we move onward in our earthly existence, we learn that our station in life is wholly dependent on the perception of our surroundings.

The knowledge that we create our essential being based on our inner desires is the key to grounding and happiness. The relaxation we manifest is a byproduct of our own ability to accept the reality of what truly is in the here and Now.

Be mindful of your thought's intentions, be blessed by your own higher purpose, and be well!

Teaching Moments

From our earliest memories, we have looked to our parents, teachers and friends to show us the way. The lessons we have learned by observation and interaction have shaped who we are and guided the path we travel.

The connection we feel for those who impart their wisdom to us touches us at the core of our being. These teaching moments are captured in our mind's eye for all eternity, and fill our hearts with kindness and appreciation.

The gratitude that is built through the energy exchanged in the student-teacher relationship is one that resonates deeply and can never be duplicated. Every mentor we are blessed with along the way brings with them a unique perspective and set of skills to share.

The gifts given are tools that we store away for use when the situation requires their application, knowing well in your heart that when you are ready, the teacher is guaranteed to appear. The knowledge that is in store for you depends on your need and openness to receive.

Be aligned with the presence of mind to find your educators in even the most unlikely places, be open to the lessons as they present themselves, and be well!

Your Inner Knowing

We all have within us a light, and its brilliance shines from our soul. This inner strength is drawn from the source, but only radiates with our inner acceptance.

The knowledge that you can accomplish the goals in your heart is the key to the manifestation of your life's plan. There is no earthly boundary that can be set that will extinguish your internal flame as long as you stoke the fires that drive your intent.

The intentions you lay before the world is the road map you are blessed to follow. Having faith in your knowing will always serve you highest and best purpose.

Your sails are always ready to hoist to the winds. Your determination and courage are the strength it takes to make what you have in your mind's eye a reality.

Be resolute in your passion, be in alignment with your internal drive to succeed, and be well!

Inspire Happiness

The core thesis of life is to learn, and we do this most effectively through positive experiences. The highest vibration we can aspire to is that of love.

When we are on this frequency, the possibilities are endless as all of the resources of the universe are available to us. When we truly recognize that we are equipped with the tools necessary to tune our receivers to the channel of our choosing, we eliminate the need to align ourselves anywhere but to the frequency band that inspires happiness.

The joy we stimulate within ourselves is the self-induced leverage required to raise above the issues that appears to weigh us down. Know well that a genuine smile is the fastest way to raise your vibration.

This tool is the immediate power you hold within yourself to control your environment as your perception is the anchor point for your reality. Take great care to be creator of your own joy.

You are the master of ceremonies of the party you host for yourself daily. This star-studded event is the red carpet that is your life; please feel free to invite the guest stars that bring you laughter, good times and feed your soul.

Be happy, have fun, and be well!

Maximizing Love and Light

The elevation of our soul's experience here on Earth is dependent on the frequency to which we choose to attune. We are the master of our perception and that governance is the criteria that sets the path we walk.

Happiness is ours to manifest when we align our essence with the reality we create. This understanding is the fulcrum that creates the leverage we require to position our being with the joy we have in our hearts.

We have a moral responsibility to maximize the love and light in our lives and minimize the darkness and pain. This is not to say that the twists and turns along the way will not bring challenges, but we have the innate ability to rise above the fear and anxiety to make the best of any situation.

Be a positive influence on yourself and those you love, be the light that overcomes, and be well!

Expanding Our Understanding

We all have our own definition of success, and its criteria is based on our personal experiences, values and goals. The path we travel toward our desired destination is one that is founded on our freedom to choose a direction and the liberty to subscribe to the thought process of our creation.

One of the greatest pleasures we may encounter as we formulate our personal success criteria is the opportunity to participate in a wide array of activities, meet many types of people and visit unique places. Any one of these events can be life changing as we gather data and build an understanding of what truly matters to us.

As we explore what is presented to us, we expand our understanding though trial and error. This process is one that is differs from person to person based on personality, means and the path chosen.

The options that come to us are significant as variables in the equation we are solving as we balance who we are with who we chose to be. This form of karmic algebra, one that enlists all of the possibilities from the universe's source when we are open to energy as it comes to us as true wealth, is by your design and will come to in the form of your choosing.

Be open to the options as they present themselves, be in alignment with your vision of what wealth means to you, and be well!

Transcending Our Earthly Unknowing

The connection we share with the universe grants us the fortitude to transcend our earthly unknowing. This elevated vantage point affords us the courage and stamina to climb to the heights of our wildest dreams.

Deep within us all lies the key to unlock the vast power that our life plan has in store for our journey. We always have the option to accomplish what we have in our mind's eye when we open our soul to the ability we have been gifted as a birthright.

We are Spirit and our essence is the sun, moon and stars when we manifest their alignment through present thought and action. Open your psyche to the energy that surrounds you and simply be one with what you feel to be your reality.

Be conscious, be in the Now, and be well!

Act Upon Your Dreams

Every day we set forth to build something. The creations we visualize are manifested over time through our diligent efforts, interactions and passion for life.

As we amass our resources, we forge the foundation that stabilizes us, our family and circle of loved ones. This community becomes the platform from which we launch our expedition to achieve the goals we have plotted on our map to success.

The underpinnings of our communal efforts for accomplishment are based on the knowledge we have gathered and the security we have created. The understanding that we have is the foundational bedrock that grants us the starting point to focus our intentions in the direction of our dreams.

Start your day with the confidence that you have the courage to act upon your visions. Go forward without concern or regret; you have all the tools you need at your disposal.

Be in alignment with your personal growth goals, be confident in your ability to achieve them, and be well!

Communication is the Cornerstone

Communication is the cornerstone of connection, kindness and collaboration. The knowledge that our ability to align our energy with others through our expression and intentions is the conduit we rely on to bolster our emanating vibration.

Through our presence, we work to attune our frequency to those we share time and space with as we walk our path. The conscious choice we make to connect with others is the gift we share with the world.

Know in your heart that what you create energetically is worthy of your time and the effort to transfer its essence to those open to receive. The thoughts, ideals and actions you undertake to bring your visions to reality are the gifts you came here to impart.

Be clear in your expression, be expressive in your clarity, and be well!

Grounding Your Steps

The objective of life is to learn, and what better way to expand our knowledge base than to accept the fact that we have free will? The understanding that it's all a choice is the key to opening our minds to the riches the universe has to offer.

The days we have and the lessons we experience are the puzzle pieces that build the road map to our hallowed space. The path we take to return home is the sanctified journey that fills our soul and lightens our load.

Know well that every moment is a gift and this present is the greatest encouragement we can bestow upon ourselves. Use your faith to ground your steps as you move forward toward what you create in your mind's eye.

The manifestation of your energy's fortitude is the opus of your ability to let go and simply be one with your reality. Cherish what comes and nurture it with your full intent.

Be enamored with what you bring into existence, be content with your creations, and be well!

Step Outside

The source of our power is our ability to let go. The freedom to experience life as it comes is the catalyst for the manifestation of our thoughts into our reality.

When we open ourselves to the moment-to-moment interaction with our fellows, we allow for infinite possibilities to come into existence. The intersection of our life's path with others' journeys pierces the personal veil and cross-pollinates ideas and potential outcomes.

Stepping outside of your comfort zone to welcome in the newness of change ignites the fires that strengthen our soul's core. The excitement that awaits us all on new adventures is the very reason we are here: to learn, to grow and to cherish what we do so we may share it with those we love.

Know well that your journey will take you to places unknown. The exploration itself is the prize and you are the benefactor of all that is revealed along the way.

Be a conduit for energetic interaction, be at peace, and be well!

Soulful Essence

Our bodies and minds are designed as the middleware that bridges the gap between Heaven and Earth. As we interact in the manifested plain of existence, we serve as an antenna for the light to shine though us from the unmanifested zero-point field.

The energy we radiate is the contribution we share with the world. The opportunity to attune to the frequency of kindness and compassion is always ours for the choosing.

Know in your heart that you have the ability to rise above the common baseline of fear and anxiety that permeates most of society. Making a conscious effort to live in the present moment allows for you to channel your focus on what you know to be happy and healthy.

Be the light that leads the way for all open to its brilliance, be the avenue that connects soulful essence with the courage required for transcendence, and be well!

Practical Mastery

Our lives are a cavalcade of experiences that are all custom designed for our development. The formal education we receive in a classroom setting is merely one part of the journey.

Teachers come to us when we are ready to receive the knowledge they have to impart. They cross our paths from every possible venue; their goal is to aid us in the expansion of our understanding and belief system.

Our mindset is the key to our ability to receive what our chosen instructors have to offer. When we are open to our own transcendence, we beckon in the deeper understanding that is ours for consumption.

The ability to augment formal education and with the lessons life offers us daily is practical mastery. The acknowledgment of what is laid before us to absorb is all it takes to manifest your own destiny.

Be open-minded, be kind to all you encounter, and be well!

Removing the Shackles

The connection we create with our surroundings is the mooring point we use to ground our souls and open our minds. The relationships we build and the awareness we accept becomes the path we walk.

The universe is as complex or simple as we desire. The understanding that life contains within it the beauty and compassion of our manifestation is the key to awakening.

The interdependence we share is the bond that transcends. The human heart has within it the capacity to flourish when its shackles are removed and the energy of loving kindness leads the way.

Be blissfully present in your experience, be aligned with the grander scope of it all, and be well!

Acceptance of Our Understanding

From childhood, we have a vision in our mind's eye of how our life is supposed to be. That visualization is our roadmap, and our quest is to bring that imagery to life.

Our youth sees the world through an unfiltered lens as we experience what life has to offer. The lessons along the way build our perspective as we hone in on our desired destination.

The key to contentment is to use the knowledge learned along the way to grow and rise above concerns and fear. The acceptance of our understanding is our grounding point and this stabilization is the gift we grant ourselves rather than reacting to random external stimuli.

Allowing your energies to flow with the moment-to-moment journey raises your vibration while opening your psyche to clarity and connection. This state of being aligns with your higher purpose, attracting prosperity, knowing well that the wealth of your childhood is never lost, it's yours for all eternity.

Be at ease in yourself, be true to your vision, and be well!

Ideas and Interactions

Our lives are neatly contained within the vessel that carries and shelters us on our journey. This shell was imparted to us for our safekeeping as we explore the path we have before us.

We are first and foremost charged with our own betterment, so we may have the great honor of loving and caring for others at the height of our ability. Allow yourself the courage to accept what you know is best for your own growth and happiness as you soulfully embrace your fellows in the process.

Know well that what is best for you may not always resonate with others in your purview. The greatest gift you can share with your fellow travelers is that of your acceptance of their life course as your paths meet.

We are all here to learn, and these experiences are best facilitated by the cross-pollination of ideas and interactions. You being who you are is best served by allowing others the same respect so harmony can be achieved.

Be your own highly respected self, be the grand supporter of other's desired manifestations, and be well!

One Lesson to the Next

Our lives are intended to create a framework for our experiential existence. Through our journey, we gather the knowledge we require to fulfill the lessons we came seeking.

The path is not always clear, and the teaching not necessarily simple. The complexity of what is laid before us depends on our willingness to learn with an open heart and mind.

Acceptance is at the root of the process. The receiving of what comes before us without limitations or preconceived notions allows for an ease of transition from one situation or environment to another.

Energy flows like water, and the metamorphosis that occurs in us during transitions mirrors the same process. As we move from one lesson to the next, our frequency aligns with the power you grant it.

Know in your heart that what comes to you is for your highest and best purpose manifesting your active participation in the roads you travel. The pace is yours to set as you move from one energetic gateway to the next.

Be aware of the course you plot, be in alignment with your purpose, and be well!

Signals and Milestones

The key to a happy and successful existence is trust. Faith in the safety and symbiosis of our surroundings, family, friends and personal abilities is at the core of our well-being.

The knowledge that you are self-sufficient in mind, body and spirit is the anchor we all require to stabilize our presence. Allowing intuition to guide our way is the height of letting go and trusting the path of our creation.

Our lives are full of signals and milestones that are all sent to us to aid us on our journey. These sign posts are not always obvious, but are ever-present on the road.

Being mindful of what is shared with us as life's lessons are the fulcrum by which we grow and expand our consciousness. Listen well to your inner voice; it will always be in alignment with your life purpose.

When something doesn't feel right, then it is not. Trust your inner feelings as your personal gospel and act without compunction in accordance.

Be true to your knowing, be open to your awareness, and be well!

Your Heart Governs Your Experience

When we look at our lives and what really matters to us, we come to the realization that it's not what we have, but what we feel that dictates our happiness. The knowledge that what we think is the inward perception of the outward stimuli we absorb is the grounding we manifest for our personal safety and security.

As we interact with our fellows, we learn that the relationships we build open the doors to the pathways between the hearts we love. The acceptance that we must rise above all earthly disconnection grants us the ability to walk these hallowed grounds.

Know well that what you hold to be true in your heart is what governs your experience. The kindness and compassion that emanates from you soul attunes your vibration to the sanctified frequency we call love.

Be soulful in your presence, be compassionate with your energies, and be well!

The Space Between the Resting and Waking Worlds

There is a gift that awaits us in the morning as we awake: a gift of awareness. This knowing is one that acknowledges the space between the resting and waking worlds.

The understanding that the abstract time in the first moments when you are returning from your dream state is one that allows you to have one foot in both states of consciousness. This ability to conjoin the manifested and unmanifested realms brings with it the power to call into action the universe's source database with great ease.

Utilizing this actionable information at the onset of your day grants you the ability to shape your goals and their outcomes by merely setting your intentions. The influence your thoughts hold is infinite and their invocation is yours to summon.

This ritual is one that if done regularly will enrich your grounding and solidify your desired outcomes. The world is not a black box; we must simply look inside ourselves for the instruction manual to demystify the mechanics.

Be one with your mastery, be resolute in your understanding, and be well!

Elevate the Space Around You

The greatest gift we have in our lives is our connection to the environment in which we reside. The understanding that our essence is an essential part of the grander scheme of things is the grounding on which we can always depend.

The spirit within us is the earthly manifestation of the universal energy that permeates the world we know. As we open our hearts to the grandiose scope of what is available to us, we begin to bask in the endless possibilities.

The core of what we experience is tied to our life plan, and this roadmap is ever-present to guide us on our journey. The benevolence we feel in our soul is the mirror image of what reflects back on us when we are aligned with the frequency of compassion.

Know well that you are worthy of your best being, and when your relationship to your eternal self is conjoined with your highest and best purpose, magnificence becomes the norm. Through this symbiosis your soul is nurtured and your vibration elevates the space around you.

Be the personification of kindness, be the conduit for caring to prevail, and be well!

Life Itself is on a Need-to-Know Basis

The path we walk is one that empowers us through constant foraging, pondering and interaction. The deeper we search for our destination, the closer we get to the understanding that the journey itself is the opportunity to expand and flourish.

As we accept that life itself is on a need-to-know basis and that there is not the certainty of our master plan's success, we are afforded the ability to settle in for the experience without expectations. The letting go is the leverage we all need to maximize all of the benefits the universe has to offer.

When we surrender our need to control, we climb into a true position of strength and understanding. The epiphany that awaits us all is in the core of our being; a profound knowing that we know nothing, but yet we have access to everything.

Know well that this vast unmanifested database contains everything we require to not only be successful, but to be happy. The connection that is made when we let go of outcomes allows for the source to flow freely without limitations.

Be in the moment, be free-flowing, and be well!

Give Freely of Yourself

The compassion we have in our hearts is the energy we have to share and shelter those around us. This umbrella of energetic love is the emanation of our intent and the sincere understanding of the grander scope of what truly matters and connects us all.

As we walk the Earth, we encounter many souls, all on their own journeys. The bridges we take from one experience to the next are the frequency adjustments we make to align our vibration to those we are blessed to meet along the way.

The openness we allow to our fellow travelers is the gift we share of our own essence. When we give freely of ourselves, we build bonds that enhance the collective.

Know well that when your actions are soulful they will touch others at their core. The path we walk is elevated to its highest and best purpose when altruism illuminates the way.

Be the shining star others can follow, be kindness incarnate, and be well!

Attract Your Likeness

Our feelings and true intentions are the source of the frequencies we emanate. This patterning is the vibrational baseline that sets the stage for our interactions with our fellows and the bricks we lay for the path we travel.

The knowledge that we control our destiny is all the power we require to achieve what we see in our mind's eye. No matter how large or small the goal may be, we may rest assured that when we approach any endeavor with gratitude, the universe will return that kindness with a like response.

As we move down the road of our creation, there is an amplification that takes place. This intensification of our life force is the energetic swell that we surf on a daily basis.

This heightened sense of awareness affords us the understanding of our positioning and influence on the world in which we exist. This great climb is our life's journey and with the assistance of those we meet, greet and hold dear, we build a circle of compassion that shelters and nurtures us.

This space holds within it a light that shines bright and welcomes all in its image. Greatness, like beauty, is in the eye of the beholder.

Take comfort in knowing that the imagery you manifest will broadcast on your frequency and attract its likeness in kind. Your gratitude is a beacon; a light to illuminate the way and attract the kindness you desire.

Be compassionate, be grateful, and be well!

The Pathway Home

Our ability to give of ourselves freely to those we love is the root of our consciousness. At the base of our being resides the connection to the grander purpose we are here to serve.

Through service, we align our souls with the collective force that bonds us all. As we open our minds to the larger picture, we feel the loving energy at our core exceed the boundaries of the cadre of people we hold close.

As we develop our awareness, we elevate our vibration to include all within our purview. Through this understanding, we sanctify the energetic relationships we draw to us.

This exchange of life force crumbles exterior walls as a symbiosis is born. The ability to nurture those in our circle and beyond becomes the focus of our existence.

Be the one who freely gives time and spirit, be the pathway others follow home, and be well!

Seeing Above the Veil

If we look at our lives as a personal project to be managed, time can be viewed as the linear measurement used to baseline scope and accomplishment. From childhood, we are taught that we are going to go to school, then work, and then grow old and die.

Is this all there really is? If you look at life through the lens that is presented to us in the traditional sense, then this plotted course may be all you see in front of you.

I would like to offer an alternate perspective. This "B-Side" to that record of life is one that eliminates the linear viewpoint and substitutes the expansiveness that the energy of the present moment brings to the table.

There is no set course, no right or wrong way to go about life; there are only the decisions you make in the Now that work as building blocks for the road you are paving for yourself and those you care about. Letting go of the anchoring concept of time releases you to infinite possibilities.

The finish line disappears as we reset our success criteria to disregard the fear of death from our lexicon. We are never limited by anything; limitations are self-induced shackles that can be shed by your own choosing.

Know well that growing old is a not a foregone conclusion. Old is a state of mind that need not exist. Your longevity and well-being is established in purpose and connection to those you love and the goals you continue to set.

Be youthful in spirit and deed, be open to seeing above the veil, and be well!

The Internal Compass

We all have an internal compass that is our litmus test for how we interact with the world at large. This factory-installed piece of equipment is generally the guardrail that keeps us on the road and in the proper lane.

Know well that you have this inner voice that allows for the use of the autopilot function if you open your mind and listen clearly to the downloads without distortion. Step back and isolate your perspective so that you can see it through the lens that is your own.

If something comes to you, it has purpose. Allow acceptance of your own sense of right and wrong to be your guide as there is no truer source.

Be cognizant, be diligent, and be well!

The Vessels We Seek

So much of our life is spent waiting for the next opportunity to arise or a sign post to present itself. The reality is that the empty spaces that we often discount as the questions in our lives are in fact the vessels for the answers we seek.

When we look deep within the darkness, we find ourselves. The awareness that comes to us is the understanding that we hold as the ability to create the life we wish to experience.

Embrace the unknown as the placeholder for the insertion of the being we choose to manifest therewithin. The dance we call living is in perpetual motion, and we never tire when we are open to the energy as it presents itself in its full grandeur.

Be the embodiment of the excitement you have in your soul, be the exuberance that you know to be you, and be well!

Innate Intelligence

The world in which we live is a vast intersection of all types of reality and overlapping belief systems. To the discerning participant, the experiences we encounter are built on an understanding that there is more than what just meets the eye.

The key to our success as individuals is dovetailed with that of the collective. The acceptance that we are merely one instrument in the symphony that is the soundtrack for all existence is the vantage point that puts it all into perspective.

Reconciling our place in the world is the threshold to awareness. Knowing that you are never being asked to do more than you can allows for the peace of mind and the courage that enables us to thrive.

The universe has an innate intelligence that can be counted on to support those who allow the gears to turn and the machine to flourish. This microcosm that is your life is in direct correlation with the encompassing macro environment.

The machine that is the universe is in need of your services, all while being a self-contained and fulfilling system. There is a symbiosis in cause and effect that governs the omnipresent mechanics, and it will march on to protect the whole at all costs.

Be part of the concerto, be open to the music we generate together, and be well!

Transcending Individualism

The greatest responsibility we have as human beings is to recognize the interrelationship that we have to one another. Through this understanding, we come to the reckoning that our actions, thoughts and goodwill create the energetic connection that manifests the frequency of the environment in which we live.

The alignment we create through the bonds of interaction stimulates the patterns that bring life into being. The process we call living is an expansive organism that transcends individualism.

As we travel through our days, we build what we perceive as our personal existence. Through this facade, our essence becomes one of the components of the grander scheme.

Know well that you are here to make a difference, and the choice is yours as to what heights you wish to soar to. Hold those you love close while saving space for the others who you will develop a synchronicity with at a later date.

Be giving with your life force, be a charitable messenger for Spirit, and be well!

The Simplicity of Being

Our journey is an amalgamation of the micro and macro facets of our personal complexity. The linear experiences we encounter are blended with non-sequiturs to create what we refer to as life.

As we celebrate our big wins with all of the passion that they are due, there is a tendency to overlook the ordinary. There are many days that bring with them the simplicity of being.

This gentle wave of existence is the true essence of opportunity. The days that present themselves as open prospects with no affixed agenda are the open spaces we leave for wonder to cross our path.

The amazement that is poised to walk in through this open door is one that may be epic in proportion, or may be a kindly small gesture with its focus on your well-being and tranquility.

Budget your time, energy and space to be aware of the vast potential in the smallness of it all as the micro contains within it the DNA that shapes the universe. It's up to us all to recognize the beauty for what it is when it presents itself in its multitude of forms, shapes and sizes.

Be a champion for kindness, be in control of your perspective and be well!

The Kindness You Show Yourself

Our greatest asset is that of our own well-being and happiness. As the stewards of this essential commodity, we must look deep within ourselves to gain an understanding of what it takes to maintain the life force we require to support our basic needs.

The ability to put one's welfare in a hallowed space is the key to living a fulfilled existence. As we mature, our requirements change to support the life we choose to live.

At the root of our being is a need for connection to the others around us. To maintain these relationships we must nurture not only the symbiosis we create, but our physical and mental health as well, allowing our best self to prevail.

Please know that your essence is steeped in the kindness you show yourself and through this gift you gain the fortitude to aid others on their paths. We are always as benevolent as we choose to be to the world we inhabit.

Be the goodness you know from source, be the empathy the world requires to raise the collective vibration, and be well!

Education, Exhilaration and Expansion

Life's journey is intended to be a wild ride that educates, exhilarates and expands your perception through your experiences and revelations. Know well that the path of your choosing is one that that fortifies the goals you have contracted yourself to achieve.

The mission you have set out to accomplish is the focal point of your being. The genesis of this central focus is something deep within you; something that calls to you from your energetic origination point.

Looking deeply into your own eyes in the mirror's reflection is a window to your soul and a roadmap to your destiny. Every day when you wake, take the time to set your intentions to realize the vision you have for the remarkable life you are manifesting.

This world is yours for the creation. The knowledge that you are the artisan and a masterpiece is yours for the making is the key to happiness and success.

Be extraordinary, be aligned with something bigger than yourself, and be well!

Self-Actualizing Power

There is an unseen connection between our thoughts and our internal body chemistry. The link that exists is the manifestation of our very essence.

As we perceive the world around us, we attune to the frequency of our mind's eye. Through this understanding, we build the foundations that align our physical existence with our state of mental well-being.

Know well that our environment is of our perception's making both inside and out. The expansive opportunity is always at our ready to open our souls to happiness where the body will follow in close proximity.

Our being is the mirror of our desires and this process is an infallible reality. Opening your mind to the self-actualizing power you hold is the key to unlocking the full opportunity to live the life you choose for yourself.

Be the health you know to be within you, be the happiness at your core, and be well!

The Simplicity of What You See and Feel

We all have a purpose; a goal to fulfill. On some levels, we come with it hardwired like the firmware on our computers, and as we experience what life has to offer, we fine tune and upgrade as we mature.

The knowledge that we are not alone lends to the understanding that our focus may not always be of a personal agenda. Our desired sphere of influence may very well overlap with that of others on a similar trajectory.

When we seek to serve something higher than ourselves we see beyond the veil that separates us. Knowing well that our bodies are merely vessels that create the mobility in our experience, we learn to nurture this physicality all while striving for the deeper connection to well-being though our understanding of universal mechanics.

Our physical and unmanifested connection to our environment is one that sees us as energetic beings. The universe is viewed by most as a black box with very little understanding of how all components interrelate.

When we allow ourselves to connect more deeply with the interwoven fabric of the universe we are able to draw from its source. Step away from what you have always thought you knew and open your thoughts to the simplicity of what you see and feel.

This unfettered access to the grander power source will raise the bar for what you are capable of achieving for yourself and others. Know this in your heart so you may connect with those who require your support.

Be aware of something bigger, be open to miracles, and be well!

Building the Roads

As we look profoundly into the depth of the questions that surround our very existence, we open the doors to the pathways that lead us to the manifestations of our perception. Through these adventures we welcome new energy to fill our souls.

The courage we depend on is the joy we find in the essence to which we align. Know well that you are yet to acquire all the knowing you will, but you always have the tools to build the roads to the oracles you seek.

The grandeur of it all lies in the empty spaces that look to you to shine your kindness and compassion upon to bring them to life. The beacon of your heart light brings with it all the illumination that is ever required.

Embrace the mystery that your journeys encounter with a joyful demeanor. The travels you enjoy are your life's plan in action.

Be the bravest you can be, be the kindest traveler along the way, and be well!

Who You Are and What Purpose You Serve

We all tend to measure our well-being against a myriad of personal and professional factors. The stimuli that creates perception is the embodiment of the inputs of our surroundings coupled with our subsequent responses.

The need to feel safe is omnipresent. The quest for security becomes a personal holy grail as all roads lead to our hopeful fulfillment on this journey.

Know well that contentment is an internal knowing of who you are and what purpose you serve. There is no earthly place or amount of money that can bring you to this deeper, self-created sanctuary.

Look no farther than your internal resources to feel at ease. Trust your path and its interconnections to provide you the understanding required to grant what you seek.

Be at ease, be fluid in your space, and be well!

The Ability to Shape Reality

We must be ever mindful that the energy we exude is the frequency to which we align our thoughts and their power to create. The essence we manifest in word and action are the prevailing byproducts of the perceptions of our mind's eye.

As we interact with the partisans of our experience, we are gifted the exchange of communal life force. This mana is the incantation we share with the world though our utterances.

The ability to shape reality is firmly within our grasp. Know well that what you say casts the spell that grants you access to the path you state.

The grand choice is always yours to govern. Work hard to be vigilant with your speech, as it holds within it the majestic force to build or destroy based on the intent you bestow upon its vibration.

Be attentive to your tongue, be the ambassador for great beauty, and be well!

The Knowledge of Who You Are

The knowledge of who you are is the anchor point on which you rely for grounding and stability. This understanding is derived through the work done to create a conscious perception of ourselves and the environment in which we reside.

As we move through our days, we are insightful beacons emanating the vibration of our choosing. The opportunity is ours to manifest a frequency that resonates with our grand plan for success and happiness.

This roadmap marks the milestones on the path as well as guides our interactions with our fellow travelers. The voyagers we encounter are mirrors presented to us to reflect and remind us of our inner character and outward appearances.

Granting yourself the kindness of heart to be mindful of what you see as your reflection is the wisdom you bestow upon yourself and your fellow emissaries. Know in your heart that what you hold dear is your true north.

Be aligned with your purpose, be compassionate, and be well!

The Duality of Our Path

We all play a part in the great experience we call life. The roles we assume on the surface are personal and self-serving, while in reality there is an interconnection that bonds us all at the molecular and cosmic levels.

The duality of our path is one the connects our mind, body and soul. As we walk the Earth, we learn and grow at the pace that suits our highest and best purpose.

Know well that your vibration is one of your creation, and your spirit aligns with the life you manifest. The environment in which you reside is the protoplasm from which you draw life-sustaining energy, and in turn, you share your magical essence with the collective.

Strive to be the best you can be, physically and emotionally, as your well-being sheds light on the others in your life. Our best is the wind in the sails that propels the collective to its greatest possible heights.

Be you in your grandeur, be the fascination that is a cog in the karmic mechanism, and be well!

Our Calling Card

While our mood is our calling card to the outward world, its alignment with our inward self in its true existence is the key to good health and stability. The connection between what you feel and what you allow others to see is the gauge by which you can measure your well-being.

Societal standards generally dictate our interactions with our fellows. This commonality of what is acceptable is a schema designed to create a homogeneous environment.

This surface level world is one that can best be summed up in this exchange between two people: "How are you?" "I'm well, thank you for asking."

The above is nothing more than an extended hello. Ninety-nine percent of the time, this interaction is shared by people who are merely acting out what is expected of them.

Therein lies the issue. If we are expected to be part of a group, then how can we function in a healthy light if the majority of our actions are superfluous at best? The key to being in a good mood is sincerity of heart.

If you are free to express yourself, then making the decision to be in a good mood is as simple as taking a breath. Self-induced censorship is destructive to not just yourself, but the world in which we live and to be avoided whenever it is possible for the common good.

Be the light in your well-being, be honest with yourself, and be well!

You Are Right Where You Are Supposed to Be

The key to success is to allow yourself to accept what is. The knowledge that the wheels of life are in constant motion, propelling us forward in alignment with our master plan, is the essence that sustains our well-being.

As hard as we may try there is no way to control all of the moving parts that complete us. Letting go and gifting trust to the universe is the symbiosis that frees the tumblers of time, space and reality to work their magic.

Know in your heart that you are right where you are supposed to be. The acceptance of this fact melts away the stress that we create when we hold on too tightly to what we think should be our present moment.

Open your soul to what is presented to you. The experience you will create is one of ease and comfort that will lead you to the peaceful existence you seek.

Be the catalyst for your own happiness, be patient with your own process, and be well!

Trust in What You Know - Know in What You Trust

As we awake from our night's travels to our dream state, we are faced with the beauty of the day and all of the tasks we have awaiting our attention. Take those first moments to ground yourself in the energy that is your existence.

Be kind to yourself and do not rush into flight. Set your path with the intentional manifestations in your mind's eye.

The course is yours to map, and the engagement begins when you set out to accomplish your desires. Step out into the day with the knowledge that you have the tools and ability to make it all happen.

Trust in what you know. Know in what you trust.

Be the motivation that carries you and others forward, be the energy that powers goodwill, and be well!

Debits and Credits

The routines of our lives can be accounted for energetically, like the debits and credits in a general ledger. The currency reported in this treatise is our most precious commodity, and we must take great care to be judicious in its use and application.

We all approach personal and professional tasks with our own unique sense of urgency. These calls to action all bring with them a hierarchical rhythm that sets tempo and prioritization.

Any given success criteria by definition brings with it a need to define a satisfactory conclusion. This desired end point can be reached through a multitude of paths.

The path to completion may be reached over time or in a big bang fashion. When the tally is taken and the books are closed, the results will clearly show that the slow and steady approach will have expended less personal effort and created a lower level of collateral damage on those around us than the alternative brute force method.

Be the mindful steward of your accounts, be conservatively kind with your energies, and be well!

Trust in Yourself to Bridge the Gaps

We walk the Earth with an innate knowing that we are here on a quest, and that understanding stirs deep within our being. The feeling that we are alone on our journey is an illusion to be transcended.

Throughout our lifetime, we look overtly to others to guide and enlighten us as we mature and gain faith in ourselves. The path we take is the one we manifest of our own volition and free will.

Look no farther than who you see in the mirror to be your guru and teacher. You have the tools within you to lead you to the destinations in your mind's eye.

Your expeditions will connect you with the souls and lessons you seek to complete your plans. Trust in yourself to bridge the gaps as you come to them, connecting you to the source that makes us all whole.

Be the master and the student of your intent, be the bonding that solidifies who you know yourself to be, and be well!

Life on Earth

Life on Earth is a constant barrage of sensory inputs that have the ability to overclock our bodily systems and tax our souls. The understanding that we have limits to what we can ingest physically and emotionally is the first step in building a sustainable framework for positive manifestation.

This grander understanding of actual limitation creates a scope for our usable bandwidth that maps out the boundaries that require our vigilance. These markers are the milestones that notate the path to our inner being.

This sacred space is the deepest connection to the universal source, and it can only be reached by the sheer collapse of what binds our being to the physical realm. As we ascend the ladder of understanding, we come to realize that to get to a place of peace we must allow for loving energy to flow freely to our core.

This openness in time, space and perceived reality is achieved through meditation and letting go of what you think you know. All of the wonders of the universe are accessible through the portal of your mind's eye.

Be open to your own counsel, know you are never truly sitting alone, and be well!

Devotion to the Whole

The home we call Earth is designed to be our playground and test bed for growth and development. As stewards of this space, we must look to one another to maintain the environment in which we reside.

The physical landscape, as well as the life sustaining energy fields, require our attention. Devotion to the collective we call home is the nurturing springboard to universal transcendence.

We all draw life sustaining power from the collective, and we must be mindful of the symbiosis that is our essence. Look within to connect to the source through meditation and prayer, and then focus your attention outwardly to give back.

Follow your inner calling to draw you to the knowledge you need to do your part. Your mindful acceptance of your role is all that is expected of you.

Be an active participant in your realm, be loving in your stewardship, and be well!

Harmonic Chords

Our feelings and emotions are the sensory overlays we use to gauge and guide our well-being. These harmonic chords are in alignment with our surroundings and the elements of our purview.

The choice is ultimately ours as to how we wish to interact. Options are the key to free will, and we are never at a loss to have the ability to enlist our deeper powers of understanding to assimilate or repel what is laid before us.

We all spend our lifetimes amassing the knowledge necessary to choose our path. This emotional highway is as wide open or as closed off as you wish it to be.

The forks in the road come often, some with obvious destinations and others more obscure, but all with the pending consequence of the direction you elect. Know well that the power is within you to manifest the outcome of your choosing.

Be optimistic about what you encounter, be aligned with joy, and be well!

Embrace the Calm

As we experience the waking moments of our lives, we come to realize that the haste we create is a byproduct of our disconnection with our inner self. We are here to learn through doing and the greatest lesson we are taught is that there is an appropriate time for action, and there is also a suitable time for inaction.

When we settle our perpetual movement to a state of rest, we align our essence with the energy that surrounds us. The life force that sustains us is contained within the invisible power grid that is our world.

Look no farther than you where you sit to gain perspective and connection to what truly is reality. This gift to yourself opens your spirit to embrace the calm as your grounded state of being.

Be at ease in your own tranquility, be accepting of your abilities, and be well!

Life's Bubble Wrap

Our lives are a series of events that are designed to work toward the maturing of our body, mind and soul. This path is one that is the experiential adventure that nurtures the journey from infancy to adulthood.

We start life with some semblance of the guardrails that our parents create, and as time passes, life's bubble wrap is peeled away, exposing our psyche to the opportunity to learn and grow without the limitations of the protective buffer. As the occasions present themselves, the lessons increase in scope and magnitude.

We all started as a fully dependent creature, and with the seasoning life on Earth offers us, we all have the ability to become the alpha prototype for our own troop. This path is one that sees the progression from needing to providing, from student to teacher, and from amazement to reverence.

Know well that the bumps and bruises are by design, and the pain and discomfort is to create the juxtaposition between living and learning. Life is a heroic education, and every moment is to be cherished, catalogued and put to use for your own betterment.

Be confident in your acceptance, be at peace with the road traveled, and be well!

Improvisation

We are poised day in and day out to be the main character in the one man/woman improvisational act we call life. The stage is set and the crew is always here to support the endeavors that we bring to reality.

When we interact with situations as they present themselves, we hone our skills and deepen our understanding. The knowledge base we expand is founded in our ability to accept events as they come, and how they play into the scope of our responsibility to our master plan.

Look within to fully grasp the lessons as the present themselves. The outward stimuli is simply the window dressing on what you know to be the portal within you to the deeper meaning you are here to experience.

The world is as beautiful or as unforgiving as you allow it to be. The perceptions you manifest are yours to call into being.

Be ever-vigilant in your self-awareness, be accepting of circumstance, and be well!

The Fears We Overcome

Our lives are our worlds, and their experiences are of our creation. We own this path and must take great pride in what we bring into existence.

Our goals and aspirations come encoded for trial and error. The process is an experiment that has no foregone conclusion.

The joy we manifest is derived from the fears we overcome. Look within yourself to gain the faith required to be the purveyor of your innate goodwill, empathy and courage.

Look to the heavens for what you came here knowing. Look within for the connection beyond the space without.

The life we live is the embodiment of our perceptions and collective actions. This knowledge is never wasted, and always available to those open to receive what is gifted from the source.

Be aligned with what you feel to be righteous, be compliant with your inner voice, and be well!

Many Stations Unknown

We are a minute-to-minute, evolving work in progress. The acceptance that we are never done learning is the positive energy that facilitates the growth and change in our lives that anchors the tracks leading to many stations unknown.

Knowing well that our course's guaranteed variations open the spectrum of possibilities for us and others, we map out our journey based on what we accept as truth and leave the rest to providence. The environment that surrounds us is one in which we inhabit as well as create.

Our energies, intentions and efforts shape the landscape for ourselves and our compatriots. Our ultimate goal goes deeper than simply the betterment of ourselves and our position in life.

What is bestowed upon us is the opportunity to enhance the experience for the collective. This broader practice is one that you have the ability to pass on to future generations as you raise the ocean for all.

Be open to change, be aware of growth, and be well!

Plant Your Roots

The connection we feel to our environment is the source of energy we draw from to power our minds, body and soul. We build shelters that protect our well-being, and these structures are of both a tangible and intangible nature.

We must work hard to acknowledge and accept our space in the universe. The knowing that we are part of the natural flow is the key to finding your way with grace.

Grant yourself the poise to align with the universal mechanics that maintain harmony and balance in our world and beyond. The knowledge that our surroundings are not foreign to us is the lynch pin to transcending the fear of what we cannot control.

Opening your heart to the omnipotence of the mastery that universally exists is the catalyst for the transformation required to live in peace with yourself. Home is where you plant your roots, and roots are defined by your grounded ability to find solace in your existence.

Be the calm that opens your eyes to what can and cannot be seen, be conscious of your breath and its governance, and be well!

The Omnipotent Repository

The world we live in is the user interface to something much deeper. The thoughts and actions we present in this space are effectively queries we make to the back end of the universal database.

In quantum physics, this omnipotent repository is referred to as the zero point field and its power is readily accessible to us all. With this knowledge in mind, please pay close attention to your thoughts as the controlling mechanism for your environment.

It truly is as simple as working the remote control for your TV, or asking Siri or Alexa to play the music of your choice. What we perceive is reality and what manifests as your truth becomes the mantra for the experience at large.

Staying in an optimistic frame of mind elevates your frequency, allowing others of a heightened awareness to enter your space and influence your path in a beneficial way. This engagement induces the symbiosis of positive thoughts and deeds.

Be confident in your knowing, be open to the insights all around you and be well!

The Power to Create

The power to create lies within us all. Please know well that every one of us has access to the source that brings the essence of life to the forefront of reality as we understand it.

Look to your innermost spaces for the energy that you hold dear to bring your dreams into being. The core of your creativity stems from the knowledge that you can achieve what you set out to accomplish.

Have faith in your ability and passion to be the genesis of your soul's vision. The path you walk is the thoroughfare you have built that leads from your heart to the places that were manifested therein

Be the compassion of your self-awareness, be the charity that starts at home and leads to the roads yet to be traveled, and be well!

Your Personal Signature

We are all unique beings with our own purpose and plans to achieve the goals we seek to fulfill. The route we take to the destinations we choose is intimate to our spirit's essence.

Know well that the love you put into your actions is the governance that sets the tonality of the frequency to which you attune. This vibratory field is the aura you emanate, and in turn, the souls you attract.

The kindness and compassion you bestow on the world is your personal signature by which you are recognized. When you are sincere in your intent, your manifestations will hit their mark.

The person you choose to be is the blessing you pay forward to the incarnations yet to come. Cherish the originality that is by your design, and allow its blueprint to be shared for the greater good.

Be the light that shines as brightly as it is seen, be the goodwill that stokes the fires for all to enjoy its warmth, and be well!

Roads Peacefully Traveled

Life is a constant barrage of sensory inputs that fills our thoughts and minds with an abundance of perceptions to manage. This deluge of sights, sounds, tastes and smells is the artistic palette we utilize to manifest the experience that best suits our vision of happiness.

Know well that the senses you employ are the gatekeepers of your well-being. These receptors allow you to gauge the level of desirability of the external factors that weigh on your internal connection to the source.

As we walk through our days, we seek the best outcomes and interactions. When we steep our essence in that which we find enhances our being, we thrive, and in turn, elevate those around us.

Rely on your sensitivities to reinforce what your intuition shares with your waking presence. What you feel is what you know, and it will always lead you back to the roads peacefully traveled.

Be aware of what stimulates the joy within you, be conscious in your being, and be well!

Simply Be Yourself

Who we are is dependent on who we choose to be. Having a fundamental grasp of your purpose in life aids in the establishment of the roots that anchor you and the branches you outstretch to the world.

The environment in which we live in has a very strong polarizing ability that attempts to force people to make wholesale sweeping decisions to identify themselves with certain groups or mindsets. As individuals, we only need to be recognized for our actions.

We are free to associate as we choose with the openness of mind to create our persona based on the best of all we have had the honor to connect with along the way. The creation of who we are is a lifelong pursuit that takes many twists and turns as it works toward an eventual finished product.

The purpose of life is to experience, learn, grow, and then help others on their journey. Knowing clearly that just being yourself is all that is ultimately expected of you is a fact that relieves the pressure and elevates the soul to its rightful vantage point.

Simply be yourself. Know well you have spent a lifetime gathering what you need to be the best you possible!

Be self-aware, be self-actualized, and be well!

Illuminating Your Path

The greatest responsibility we have is to foster our own feelings of safety and security. When we feel at ease, we are open to the vast power the universe has in store for us to receive.

Granting yourself a safe space allows for connection at the highest of levels. The possibilities above the malaise of fear are endless, and embody your life purpose.

Illuminating your path with your own kindness and compassion will ground you in presence. Focus your thoughts and actions in the Now and you will be the force nature intends you to be.

Be happy because you know who you truly are, be free of worry because you trust in your life plan, and be well!

Our Ability to Grow

As we look deeply into our own eyes, we see the reflection of the person we choose to be. The inner knowing we establish comes through our acceptance of where we are on our life's path in relation to the destination we have in our mind's eye.

There is no preordained path to achieve our ambitions. This understanding allows for our ability to grow as we experience the lessons as they come to us.

The expansion of our scope of acceptable circumstances increases over time with our venerability. The situations that vexed us in our youth become more commonplace over time, as our allowance for change becomes a tool we use to adapt to the ebb and flow of life on Earth.

Know well that we will be pushed beyond our current boundaries, and this is by design to manifest our highest physical, mental and spiritual growth. Set your intentions to clearly make your desired outcomes known to the universe.

The road you travel is yours for the creation. Taking an active role in the tempo of the journey is your obligation to yourself.

Be clear to yourself and others as to what fills your heart with happiness, be aligned in action and goal, and be well!

The Vibration We Share

The vibration we share is a conscious decision made based on perception. This energetic gift we present is a constant reminder of our power and responsibility.

Others look to us as a conduit by which to align themselves with the positive energy of the collective good. When our frequency is attuned to that of kindness, we remove barriers and open the pathways to a joyful existence.

The days you spend in compassion will resonate deeply and bring kindred spirits to your side. Open your mind, body and soul to the loving warmth that your heart propagates, and share it with all who are ready and willing to receive.

Know well the space in which you reside is a mirror of your manifested reality. This hallowed ground is yours to create and nurture.

Be an emissary for thoughtful well-being, be an ever-present force of good, and be well!

A Way of Life

The fastest way to heighten your own frequency is to smile. Knowing this allows you to be the master of your own mood as well as a beacon of light for all around you.

Being conscious of the vibration we emanate is ground zero for the responsibility to raise the bar for the world you touch daily. Sharing the kindness and love that is the essence of a smile becomes a way of life.

Know well that your actions, feeling and emotions transfer to those in your company. Being a good steward of the environment requires attention to your well-being and its effects on those you touch.

Be happy inside and out, allowing it to spring forward from your face and plant its seeds in others' space, be a lighthouse of kindness, and be well!

Quell Your Concerns

We often look to the sky for answers and divine intervention when life perplexes us. The energy we seek from the heavens is actually not above us, but it surrounds us here on Earth.

Look no farther than then those souls you call friends and family for the guidance to quell your concerns. The connection that bonds your earthbound soul group is aligned to the highest of frequencies – the vibration of energetic love.

This hallowed space is the purest form of knowledge, courage and compassion. When we allow ourselves to accept the gift of Spirit into our hearts, we align with the oneness thought of as Heaven.

Be the magic that transcends, be the hand that is outstretched, and be well!

Classroom Constructs

Teachers, like lessons come to us in all sizes, shapes and forms. The need for formal education is never to be questioned, as the instruction gained in this format educates the traditional student in fundamental structures and accepted societal standards.

As we look beyond the four-walled classroom construct, we begin to accept the uncertainty that the world is our testing ground and this phase of life is the podium that masters ascend to in order to impart deeper knowledge and understanding. When we look around us, we have the opportunity to see the ordinary or experience the extraordinary.

This choice is a moment-to-moment opportunity to seize what is being laid out in front of us for our personal growth. We can accept the magic we see as the mastery of nature and never give it a second thought, or explore its deeper meaning and power.

Merely seeing the surface level observations inhibits the would-be student from the alchemy that surrounds us all. When we open ourselves to the wonders of what is right before our eyes, the lessons overtake our perceptions and the status of life's student is bestowed.

The teacher is life and all it has in store for you. Being in tune with your environment is the start of the marriage between your soul and the collective.

Recognizing the inherent depth of the experience opens the door, allowing the teachings to take root in your being. This metamorphosis is the beginning of the path that leads home.

Be ensconced, be aware, and be well!

The Envoy of Your Soul's Space

We all have a mission in life, and the voice we hear calls us to service. This inner knowing of what we seek is the path we walk and the destination of our choosing.

As we plot our course, we see the challenges and the joy they will bring as we persevere. The journey we embark on will see us connect with many souls along the way.

This adventure is one that affords us the good fortune to determine our own destiny through our actions and free will. As we move along through our lives, we learn the best uses for our resources as called for by circumstance.

There is a time to speak and a time for silence, a time for direct attention and a time for a more passive approach. Look deep within and embrace your intent to manifest your heart's action.

We are all here to make a difference, and the positive change we can affect is one that suits the occasion. Know well your voice will be heard if your actions align with your core thesis.

Be the envoy of your soul's space, be the light that shines from Spirit, and be well!

Mutually Beneficial Outcomes

Our will is an extremely powerful catalyst. This imposing engine is one that can be harnessed as the fulcrum for growth and advancement along our life's path.

Like with any tool, we must be mindful of its full scope of abilities to ensure the proper application of use. As we set our sights on a desired outcome, we map a course to the destination we have in our mind's eye.

While this exercise seems rudimentary for simple applications, like what is the end point for the drive we are currently undertaking in our vehicle, it is not so basic when we are dealing with the manifestation of more complex experiences. As a general axiom, we must note that when we hyper-fixate on any specific outcome, we literally work against this vison by pitting our will against anyone else who has an energetic stake in the same space.

When we rise above the outcome and accept what is produced, we allow for the natural flow to create a mutually beneficial environment. Knowing well that your energy plays a significant role in the process allows you to accept where things land as an active participant.

This letting go is the natural course in the decision-making process that requires a level of enlightenment which comes when fear and anxiety are left by the wayside. When you allow yourself to connect with your deeper understanding of well-being, the unencumbered energy of the situation flows freely, and mutually beneficial outcomes are achieved.

Be accepting, be a willing agent for change, and be well!

Look Calmly to Your Environment

We are all gifted with the life we perceive through our realization of the world around us. As we experience what our senses bring into manifestation, we awaken to the imagery we create.

The deeper we allow ourselves to connect with our surroundings, we find that our intent becomes aligned with the space in which we reside. This reality becomes the oneness that embraces and nurtures our spirit.

Look calmly to your environment to welcome you to the grand experience. The essence of the universe is as benevolent as you allow it to be.

The mastery of your imagination will be guided by your inner compassion to the green field of all karmic possibility. This journey traveled is the culmination of your life's plan, as it embodies all of your lessons learned and relationships embraced.

Be the clarity of action as it springs forth from your mind's eye, be the possibilities that see no limitations, and be well!

Maintaining Perspective and Grounding

Look no farther than your own reflection in the mirror to find your own true happiness. We all contain within us the roots that connect us to the source that nurtures our soul and provides stability and well-being.

When we focus our energy on the power of the present moment, we bypass the noise that clouds our focus and judgment. The connection we maintain to our environment is the loving warmth that we all have at our disposal to maintain perspective and grounding.

This inner link to our personal reality is the lifeline to what we hold dear. The smile on our face is simply the knowledge that our purpose is fulfilled by our very breath.

Be at ease where you stand, be the gentle hand that caresses your spirit, and be well!

Our Retrospective Heart

From the time we are young, we dream of growing up and leaving home to begin our journey to destinations yet to be known. The visions in our mind's eye were the courses we plotted to the mastery soon to be ours.

As we venture onward, we come to an understanding that what we seek is what we have always had in our retrospective heart. Home is a state of mind, and its safety and security is a comfort we create and maintain through our actions and goodwill.

Please know well that to sincerely be at peace, we must simply accept our calling to fulfill what we know to be true. The inner truth we hold dear is our personal DNA, and it is to be cherished and nurtured.

Our youth was our psyche at its purest form. Today's you is that kernel of joy with all of the enhancements you have afforded yourself along the way.

The person who looks back at you from the mirror will always be your inner child. This work of art is you as envisioned long before you set out on your expedition to explore the world and all of its possibilities.

Be at home wherever you are, be the welcoming and embracing force in the world in which you live, and be well!

The Power and Mastery of the Universe

Within us all lies the power and mastery of the universe. The inner connection we have to the source of all things is the constant that illuminates our path and opens our minds to the grandest of possibilities.

Know in your soul that your abilities are unbridled and the world's compassion is at your beck and call. We are Spirit, and this essence is the universal bond that raises our awareness when we align our being to the higher frequencies.

Set your sights on the vision you have in your mind's eye. Your dreams are your mindful internal workspace to create what your heart desires.

Rely on what you hold dear. Your passion is the drive to be what you came here to achieve.

Look to your inner faith to grant you the will to succeed. The seed is within you to nurture and bring to life.

Be the knowledge that you look upon to unlock your fullest potential, be the caregiver of your personal hallowed ground, and be well!

Life's Personal Journey

Life is a personal journey that is handcrafted by our own design. For some, there is a clear understanding of their master plan from a young age, and for others, it is the cobbling process that makes the adventure.

The joy comes in knowing the expedition is yours and yours alone to guide. There are many allies to be made along the road, but you are the master of your path and only you know where the compass of your heart leads.

Look to your inner faith to smooth the bumps along the way. Your travels are not always as kind as one would have envisioned, but your days' experiences will always work to your highest and best purpose.

Know in your heart that you know what is best for your soul's growth and Spirit is ever present along the way to sustain your well-being. You are well equipped to master the visions in your mind's eye, and the results are what your dreams were made of for as long as you could remember.

Be the curator of your own experience, be the passion that sustains the flames that light your way, and be well!

Understanding Self-Nurture

Our capability to manifest love in our lives begins with the deepest of understandings that self-nurture is the foundation of our personal well-being. The realization that we are connected energetically to our surroundings is the epiphany that unlocks the gates to the paths created in our hearts.

There are many souls we are blessed to travel with along the way, but not all are kindred spirits. Some come to us to help us with our desired lessons, and others gift us with the role of teacher, guide or confidant.

Know in your heart that every relationship brings with it the energy required to meet the need as it was intended. Look fondly on every interaction with kindness and compassion, as they are all meant to aid us on our journey.

The courage is always within us to outstretch a hand to lift others up. We must never lose sight of the fact that it is not our responsibility to alter the course of another with our will or hope to elevate their frequency.

The travels of our compatriots are their experiences, and we play a mere supporting role. There is no discredit to you or the times you have shared to part ways when an alignment no longer exists.

Be ever vigilant in steeping yourself in a positive space, be kind in your creations and be well!

Your Soulful DNA

The sincerest beauty in our lives comes from a deep understanding of who we are at our core. This connection we have with our soul's source is the earthly incarnation of our karmic design.

Know in your heart that you are that essence that you hold dear, and that your very being connects you to the universal life force that sustains and conjoins us all. Look within to ground and calm your outward existence as your life takes its shape while you reach for the pinnacle of your dreams.

You are as unique as you allow yourself to be in mind, body and spirit. Your soulful DNA is the energetic bond you create with all aspects of the world you manifest into creation.

Be humble as your inner light shines and illuminates your path and that of those blessed to be in your life, be ever vigilant in your mission to spread goodwill and kindness, and be well!

Culminating Meditation

Please sit comfortably with your feet on the floor...

Close your eyes and begin to focus on your breath, asking the protection of your angels, guides and soul groups...

As your attention drifts away from the manifested world's sights and sounds, you begin to align with your inner self's connection...

This powerful attraction to your inner essence draws you in deeper to the loving energy that surrounds and bonds us all in our earthly resonance...

Raise your hands above your head, creating an antenna to the unmanifested field of Heavenly energy...

Open your hands and adjust their spacing to receive and embrace the energy being shared from on high...

When you feel the power of the energy tingling between your hands, pull it down through your being, starting at your head's crown, working down past your forehead's Third Eye, through your throat, into your heart, down into your belly, through your sacral region and into your roots at the very base of your connection to Mother Earth...

Allow your life force to meld with all creation through your core, and when you feel your roots saturated with warmth and compassion, begin to reverse the process, pulling the Earth-infused energy back through your system, and reseed it in the heavens reconnecting you with the source...

(Repeat the process infinitely at your leisure)

About the Author

Jay was born to this incarnation with a very specific purpose as his life's calling, and to be honest, he was reluctant to return to Earth this time knowing what he did about the early stages of the journey he was to undertake. His otherworldly arrogance brought him back to a set of parents that he felt only he could help; he was soon proved to have bitten off more than he could chew.

From an early age, his plans were thwarted, as his presence did not manifest the sense of harmony he had expected in the family unit that his arrival created. He and his mother never truly bonded. While his father was a wonderful and nurturing caregiver, he was always up to some shenanigans that left his mother wondering what was really going on with their marriage. The energy in the house was never stable; in fact, it was volatile.

Jay's parents divorced when he was eight. This was a true blessing in obvious retrospect, but the shock of coming home from a summer trip between second and third grade, visiting family in the countryside of Pennsylvania, was life-changingly painful to say the least. Jay's dad, the only caregiver he had ever really known, drove off down the street after a strange family barbeque to helping his son settle back into his unexpected new life.

Jay's grandmother, knowing what was in store for her grandson when he returned to California, decided to send her boy home with a pet to look out for him. Jay brought back a Pennsylvanian kitten that was later named Jefferson, who became his familiar and confidant. This gesture by his grandmother was the first of many that bolstered their relationship and heightened their bond, while further dismissing what little connection there was between Jay and his mother.

Jay's mom knew that he needed some help to adjust, so she gave him what may be the greatest gift of his life – she took him to meditation classes where he learned how to look inward for guidance and strength. This leg up that she granted him was the beginning of his spiritual path and calling to help others with the tools he amassed along the way. He is forever grateful to her!

Through most of elementary school, Jay lived with his mother in a state of benevolent neglect, seeing his father on the occasional weekend. There was never any issue with how it was all working out; Jay innately knew his parents were doing the best they could with the tools they had. The blessing that granted stability to Jay's young life was his "God-Family" who lived across the street. His best friend and his family all but adopted Jay, teaching him the dynamic of family, faith and connection.

Later in grade school and middle school, Jay bounced between his parent's two households. His dad had remarried a young woman who did her best to augment Jay's dad's ill attempts at parenting with her own brand of authority that never truly resonated. All that said, Jay is still friends with his stepmother today, and truly thankful for the two siblings she brought into the world. Jay is very proud of them both and fully accepting of the augmented role he fills in their lives supplementing "Dad's Way".

Jay continued his meditation through high school and college, fostering continued growth and education both spiritually and intellectually. There was a long stretch where Jay planned to be a lawyer, because that was what he was told he was going to do with his life. At some point, the realization happened that being an attorney would not serve Jay's highest and best purpose, so he opted to pass on law school after he graduated from college.

Instead of law school, Jay went into business with his father. You would think that all the red flags would have steered him clear of his father's dark web, but the allure of being with his dad was too much to resist. Needless to say, the life lessons learned were costly, as Jay saw the damage his dad was really capable of inflicting on mind, body and soul.

Now knowing well that his father's path was dark, and his mother was unable to lend any emotional support, he made his own way carving a path by forging relationships, building bridges and helping who he could along the way. Spirituality remained as the cornerstone of Jay's existence. There were times where it may not have been in the forefront, but there was always a deep knowing that there was more than what meets the eye, and something much larger was in play looking out for his well-being.

Jay was blessed to meet his wife working at a summer camp where he knew she was "the one" when he brushed up against her the first time in a team-building exercise. The nurturing dynamic they have built together over the past 30 years is what Jay had in his mind's eye when he first came to Earth to help his parents. Sadly, Jay may not have been able to help his parents in the way he felt he was originally meant to, but their actions, and sometimes inactions, have gifted the how-to, and how-not-to, that continue to guide his path as Jay raises his own son into the fine man he is becoming.

Jay has had the great honor to work with some wonderful masters along the way, who have shared the attunements that have transcended his experience to that of a Level Three Reiki Practitioner, or Reiki Master. This is Jay's true calling; to heal and share the mechanics of the universe with all he can touch.

Jay has resided in Malibu, California for 30 years with his wife, Dana, where they raised their son, Tanner. Jay augments his spiritual practice with the earthly grounding of a physical workout routine that blends core focus, resistance training, stair climbing and miles of daily walking through state parks and beaches with yoga and meditation to unite mind, body and soul.

Namaste

Photo Credits

Front Cover – Dana Rubin (Arches National Park, Utah)
Design Layout by Helane Freeman
Back Cover – Dana Rubin (Malibu, California)

www.ingramcontent.com/pod-product-compliance
Lightning Source LLC
Chambersburg PA
CBHW050334010526
44119CB00004B/136